Lion Leadership: The Power of Strategy

For Bonnie and our five daughters:
Lauren, Lexi, Linsey, Leia, and London.
Thank you for teaching me how to lead.
I love all of you so much.

Lion Leadership: The Power of Strategy

Lion Leadership: The Power of Strategy

"Strategic thinking is the bridge that powerfully
connects leadership philosophy
to effective team execution."

– Mike Rodriguez

Lion Leadership: The Power of Strategy

LION
Leadership
THE POWER OF STRATEGY

MIKE RODRIGUEZ

TRIBUTE
PUBLISHING

2021

Lion Leadership: The Power of Strategy

Copyright © 2021
Tribute Publishing LLC
Frisco, Texas

Tribute Publishing, LLC

LION Leadership – The Power of Strategy
First Edition February 2021

All Worldwide Rights Reserved
ISBN: 978-1-7337727-6-1

All Rights Reserved. No part of this book may be reproduced, stored in a retrieval system, or transmitted, in any form, or by any means, electronic, mechanical, recorded, photocopied, or otherwise, without the prior written permission of the copyright owner or the Author, except by a reviewer who may quote brief passages in a review.

Printed in the United States of America.

In God We Trust.

"When it comes to leadership,
it's not the title that counts.
Are you worthy of following?"

- Mike Rodriguez

Lion Leadership: The Power of Strategy

Lion Leadership: The Power of Strategy

Introduction vii

Chapter I – Lion Leadership System of 3 1
   The Philosophy of Edwin C. Barnes 4
   Lion Leadership Philosophy 6
   Culture vs Performance 11
   Balanced vs Unbalanced Leaders 19
   The System of 3 21

Chapter II – The Power of Strategy 29
   Strategic Categories 30
   The 3 Mindsets 34
   Strategic (Cognitive) Thinking 41
   Cognitive Preparation 46
   Strategic (Active) Listening 51
   Strategic Conversations (Performance or HR) 54

Chapter III – Strategy to Evaluate Talent 61
   The KIT Car 62
   Talent Evaluation 64
   The Core 4 Strategic Components 67
   Q.E.S.T. Interview Stages 70
   Value vs Personal Worth 74
   Emerging vs Foundational Leaders 75
   The Principle of Moving People Up or Out 77

Chapter IV – Strategically Adapting to Change 81
   The M.A.I.L. Principle 82
   Using the BIG PICTURE to Lead 87
   The Paradigm Shift 89
   Recalibrate 92
   Six Foundational Leadership Truths 95

Chapter V – Sustainable Business Strategy 99
   The Word 'Impossible' 100
   Five Steps to Become More Resilient 102
   Find a Way 105
   I Challenge YOU 106
   Accept the Challenge 110
   The Final Challenge 111

Chapter VI - Tips from Lion Leaders 119
   Narrow Your Focus, Michael Trifari (President & COO, Vibe Restaurants: Little Caesars) 120
   Fundamental Principles are Core, Sasha Sigal (President, CTIconnect) 125
   Leadership Love, David Rodriguez (Owner/Operator, Chick-Fil-A) 131
   In Support of Lion Leadership, Kelly Stephens (Vice President, Engel & Volkers)...135

About the Author, Mike Rodriguez 145

Introduction

When the original Lion Leadership book came out, it was well-received by leaders in a variety of industries around the world. Due to the nature of the content, I was called on by many global organizations and names like The U.S. Government, McDonald's Corp, Chick-fil-A, Holiday Inn, and others, including many universities, churches, and companies in software and technology to teach Lion Leadership Principles. The feedback that we were given spoke directly to the fact that the principles were relevant, necessary, easy to understand and apply.

In most instances, Lion Leadership principles were a requirement for teams to apply to a broken or underperforming culture or an apathetic team. Some people reacted and disagreed with the logical approach of Lion Leadership's strategic "facts over opinions" approach, but we quickly determined that they only had opinions to share. Those people are clearly not Lion Leaders and we make no apologies for our proven principles that generate balanced results. We also quickly concluded that most naysayers had not in fact read the book, as they would know that a core principle of a Lion Leader is to avoid and negate complaining.

After countless trainings and advising sessions with our clients, I was called on to package up the broader and deeper concepts I was teaching, into this second book; *Lion Leadership: The Power of Strategy*. With that, we can reiterate profound points to you today: Lion Leadership strategies are still critical for all leaders, and in today's world, they are needed more than ever. Not only are the strategies I teach unique, but I have recognized that the basics of leadership are not being taught in the world, and in most cases, they are neglected altogether. When a leader reads, internalizes, and seeks to effectively work with their teams, the outcome becomes unlimited. During the transition process from being an emerging leader, the Lion Leader may not initially be liked. They should, however, eventually be loved. This love can only come after time, after challenges, and after tests of endurance by all members of the team. This will only happen once the team knows that the Lion Leader always has their best interest at heart.

Lion Leaders create disruptive change when necessary. People do not like change, and they will resist it. They will emotionally deflect and hide behind the false claims of their dislike for the leader, as they fight to get their own way. But what we have learned is that what they really dislike is the personal accountability to perform and the higher expectations to step outside of their mediocrity. Lion Leaders stretch comfort zones.

Whatever your current role is, know that this book will equip you to realize, learn, apply, and execute effectively as a leader. By using the strategies contained in this book, you can effectively change the outcome of your results, and the results of those trusted in your care for you to lead.

Now join me as I challenge your current thoughts, beliefs, and actions, and ask you to embrace a new way to think, as you continue your journey to become a Lion Leader.

- **Mike Rodriguez, Trainer of Lion Leaders**

Lion Leadership: The Power of Strategy

Lion Leadership: The Power of Strategy

> "Leading without establishing your leadership philosophy, is no different than living without knowing your life purpose. Both illusions lead to disaster."
>
> Mike Rodriguez

I

The Leadership System of 3

Chapter I – The Leadership System of 3

Leadership is a life-long process; you never graduate. When you started reading this book, you might not have known this, but you knew you would have to put your mind to work, so let's jump right in. Let's go back to your younger days when you actively used your imagination. Picture yourself in a large room all alone. Suddenly you look up and see me walking in through the doorway. Alongside of me walks a very large, unchained, full-maned lion. What would you do? Think about it.

If you are like most people, you would say something along the lines of "I would run, I would hide behind you Mike," or "I would freeze," or you might say something that conveys that you have decided to react emotionally out of fear. The reason most people state that they would react with fear to this hypothetical example is that they are afraid of the lion. When I hear this answer, I respond quickly and correct them by saying, "That's not true. It's not that you are afraid of the lion. You are actually afraid of what the lion can do to you." You are very aware of the power and the authority the Lion has over you.

The truth of the matter is that the lion isn't there to eat you. It might decide to eat you, but you must know that lions are strategic in their behavior. Now take note of this. If I really did walk into a room with an unchained lion that you had to face, the lion would in fact initially do one of two things:

a) **The lion would determine if you are a territorial threat.** If the lion believes you to be a threat, it would release a warning growl to alert you to back up and move away.

or

b) **The lion would determine if it is in fact hungry** and, if so, then the lion would size you up to determine if you are a viable meal. If the Lion decided it is hungry, it would then become quiet, change its posture to an attack **position** while staring directly at you. As the lion lowers

Chapter I – The Leadership System of 3

itself with its eyes fixated on you, this would be the **source** of the reality of your fear: the fact that the lion is completely in control of your life and can decide what it wants to do with you.

As we reflect on this example, the truth that can be realized is that upon the initial encounter, a lion doesn't need to growl and posture to let you know it is a lion. A lion knows it is a lion. It knows its authority and what it is capable of, and it knows that YOU know. A lion lives with disciplined strength and authority and it thinks strategically; so should you. The pride leader lives with a foundational leadership philosophy that focuses on two things:

1. Dominance and protection of the pride and their territory, and
2. Total survival of the pride. Rest, drink, hunt, eat, etc.

The power of strategy is what allows the lion and the lion pride, to survive at the top of the food chain. As a leader of people, this is this same strategic thinking that will allow you to be an effective leader and to develop effective team members for your business to survive, grow, and thrive. But we must get back to the basics. We must remember that leadership is not about position, authority, or control. Your team knows you have authority; they don't need you to remind them. Nor is your position about passive influence, timid engagement, and perpetuating an environment of weak culture, while neglecting to pursue your overall mission. Culture and performance must co-exist, results and excuses cannot. But it all starts with your philosophy to think, plan, and act with purpose.

Chapter I – The Leadership System of 3

THE PHILOSOPHY OF EDWIN C. BARNES

One of the most inspiring true stories that exists that outlines an example of deep philosophy is the story of the regular man named Edwin C. Barnes. Barnes story is about his profound dream and quest to partner in business with the great inventor Thomas Edison. There are many points to learn from Barnes story, but for the purposes of our book, we are going to focus on Barnes philosophy.

The story of Barnes shares the profound truth about his philosophy: how he viewed himself and his life, and how he took actions that reflected his philosophy. Armed with no money in his pocket, no business connections, and no relevant business skills, Barnes jumped onto a freight train to catch a ride across the country to Orange, New Jersey to meet with Thomas Edison.

Why would Barnes take such a risky, irresponsible trip? Well to begin with, it wasn't a 'trip' to Barnes, it was a required strategic step to fulfill his vision (Philosophy). The train was merely a vessel to get him to his destination to gain an audience with Edison. You must remember that to Barnes, he was being very responsible. He knew that if he didn't get on a train to go see Edison, that he would never be able to meet Edison, and therefore his dream would never come true. His dream pushed him to take action and find a way.

Once Barnes arrived in Orange, via the freight train, he went straight to Edison's place of business. He immediately knocked on the door and presented himself as he had strategically planned. Through a persistent conversation, and description of why he was there, Barnes was not only eventually able to talk with Edison, but he was also able to present his case to the inventor. "How lucky" you might say that Barnes was able to meet and present his case to Edison. I would argue that the encounter was not luck, but was rather a result of strategic thinking and actions. Think about it. Had Barnes not gotten on the train, the encounter would have never taken place (take note of this). Then you or others would have then written off his dream as being unrealistic. This is another important point. When we present our big dreams to people, they often criticize us, then, when something happens as a result of our taking action, people say that we are lucky. Remember, **if you are seeking to please people, you can never win; but when you seek to fulfill your purpose, the outcomes to win are endless.**

Edison saw what Barnes was hoping Edison would see: his determination born from his philosophy of success! The result was that Edison hired Barnes; not as his partner, but as a custodian. You might laugh, but Barnes was in, and he was now in a good position; his plan was in play. Barnes was quoted as saying:

"I came here to go into business with Edison, and I'll accomplish this end if it takes the remainder of my life."

But it wouldn't take the remainder of his life. After several years of working with Edison and working to build leadership equity, Barnes happened to overhear a meeting Edison was having with his sales team. Edison wanted to sell a new product called the Ediphone, but Edison's team wanted no part of it. They didn't believe in the product, nor did they want to sell it. Their philosophy created resistance. Seeing this as his opportunity, and believing in himself, Barnes told Edison that he would take on the product and would create the strategy to sell the Ediphone. All Edison had to do was simply approve the request. Edison approved the request and Barnes went into action.

After much hard work, success would indeed follow. As a result, Edison entered into an exclusive contract with Barnes to run Ediphone. The slogan of their new venture was "Made by Edison, installed by Barnes." With that, driven by his deep strategy to partner with Edison, Barnes had personally fulfilled

Chapter I – The Leadership System of 3

his dream. He had personally lived and experienced the power of strategy. Edwin C. Barnes had become a business partner with Thomas Edison.

LION LEADERSHIP PHILOSOPHY

When it comes to leadership philosophy, we can borrow from Edwin C Barnes. Philosophy is the thought that fuels how we think and view ourselves and the mission. Our leadership philosophy must be bigger than us or our circumstances, or we will never take action; nor will others. We must understand and adapt to the Lion Leadership philosophy.

As a lion, we must recognize our authority and our influence. We must remember that we don't need to run around telling everyone our title or bragging (growling) about who we are. It's more important to focus on how we 'view' what we are about to do. Viewpoint is truly the foundational component of philosophy that drives effective leadership. Everyone who works with you already knows your authority AND they know that you can use or abuse your authority to potentially take punitive action and end their career. They know you are the leader, and just like a lion, people know what you can do to them. Therefore, Lion leaders exercise disciplined authority. Disciplined authority is present in actual lions. You can see it when they initially evaluate a situation to determine the direction they are going to take, as mentioned above: Is this a threat, or do we need to strategically hunt?

Leadership Philosophy is the foundational element that helps us to keep our thoughts in action. We do this in order to strategically plan, so we can effectively lead ourselves and others entrusted to our care. We must own our philosophy! But first, we must understand Lion Leadership philosophy.

The Bible tells the story of a man named Saul who was called to be King, but there was a problem, Saul didn't see himself as a King. In fact, when all of the people of the kingdom were called to anoint their new king, Saul hid behind a pile of supplies. Finally, he reluctantly took his throne, but with a weak and selfish viewpoint, he became a less than desirable leader. The same Bible that tells the story of Saul, in another chapter says, "As a man thinks, so he is" (Proverbs 23:7). You may not read the Bible, but the point here is that for thousands of years, philosophy has been driving strategy.

When you mention the word philosophy to most people they immediately pause and expect you to shift into a profoundly deep conversation about ideals and truths. The truth is that philosophy is merely a word that describes the way we think about, and view things in our lives, in our society, and in our world.

When it comes to Lion leadership, and for the purpose of this book, Leadership philosophy pertains to how we view leadership. It is our thought and perspective about leading. This is critically important for all leaders, because when it comes to leadership, how we view it is typically how we do it; pertaining completely to the cognitive part of who we are. Philosophy is limited to your thoughts, your mindset, and your mental perspective.

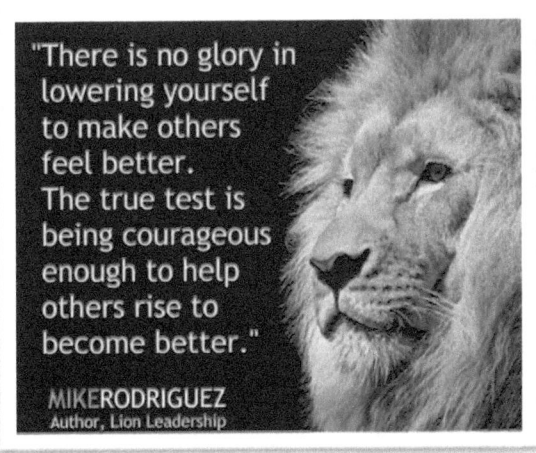

Chapter I – The Leadership System of 3

When we talk about "leadership philosophy" it is merely an abstract, personal viewpoint that most of us haven't put much thought into. Therefore, my first question for you is: **How do you view leadership, or what is your leadership philosophy?**

If you believe that having a big title makes you important as a leader, then you will be a small leader with a big ego. If leadership to you is being everyone's best friend without leadership parameters, then you will be liked, but almost certainly you will realize that at some point you have lost respect when facing difficult situations. People don't want a best friend for a leader, they want a leader who is friendly, kind, and understanding, but who is bold enough to lead them to reach the targets!

However, before you can become a great leader, you must do the hard work required of a great leader by evaluating your philosophy. For leaders, it is our vision and without it, leadership cannot exist. A Leader who operates reactively isn't a leader at all. At best they are a manager. Managers and leaders have very different philosophies about leadership. There is a big difference in managing things vs leading people and this is what separates managers & leaders. Managers "manage things," while leaders "develop people." You 'manage' your bank account, you don't lead it. You manage your projects; you don't lead them. You manage metrics and data; you don't lead them. You get the point. When you lead people, you focus **on:**

The BIG 3

    a. **Skill** – How well we do what we do and how often we take action to develop our skills. There is never a point where you max out your skills.

    b. **Resources** – are the tools that you have, how well you use them, and to the extent you use them in order to accomplish the mission. You might be provided with resources or you might have to get, find, or create them on your own (this is called initiative). **And finally….**

c. **Desire** – This is the purpose within you that drives you to use your personal gifts to pursue something greater than yourself.

Working harder doesn't create purpose. Purpose causes you to redefine how and why you work harder.

In summary, a core leadership principle that we have uncovered is that *we manage things and we lead people.* Your viewpoint of people and business is how you treat them and drive the powerful component of strategy: how you plan before you execute. However, there is a foundational challenge with leaders: most are unbalanced. Not only have most leaders neglected to evaluate their personal and team philosophy, but many more do not effectively categorize and use strategy and tactics.

Strategy vs Tactics

I often start off my leadership seminars by asking the attendees to raise their hand if they know the difference between strategy and tactics. This question often generates wide eyes that roam the room; I rarely see hands raised. The ones that are raised seem unsure and lack confidence. Besides the fact that this is a poor leadership response, I am amazed that so few people understand the differences between these core and critical leadership tools. My goal is not to bore you with academic details, so I'll explain to you as I do in my seminars:

Strategy is what happens from the neck up. It involves using the brain to formulate the plans to take action. Strategy is the thought behind the action. I say that leaders who over-strategize have big heads, not ego-wise, but they are just full of thought. You could say that they 'think' too much. (This is a character trait typically seen in the leader who always has great ideas, but never does anything about them.)

Tactics, on the other hand, are what happens below the neck. Although you can use a 'verbal' tactic, the point to remember is that a tactic is an action. I refer to leaders who use heavy tactics without strategy, as having big feet. Of course, if you have big feet and you are walking around without a strategic plan, you are going to do some significant damage. By the way, that is precisely what happens when we use tactics without proper strategies; we become ineffective, creating more damage, and our results suffer.

Strategy and Tactics are an art. Both are required for effective performance. Strategy requires time and thought to troubleshoot, mitigate risks, and align with the best possible outcomes, while tactics require time and action. Strategy and tactics are separated by "thought" and "action."

In this chapter, I am going to outline several strategies that you can start using today. Eventually, your goal should be to influence the culture and results of your organization positively.

CULTURE VS PERFORMANCE

In today's world, while most leaders clearly don't practice evaluating and implementing strategy and tactics, many more are starting to realize that something is terminally wrong. The matter at hand is that organizations have become too **culture-centric, creating an imbalance over performance.** Culture is a living breathing force that is being determined by everything that "you do" and "do not do." Culture is validated by the standards that you establish, accept, and tolerate.

Here are examples of cultural deficiencies:

Emotional Culture - This means that the leaders have shifted their philosophy to seek to chronically please the emotional wants and needs of their people, but to a fault. Although we should seek to understand and care for those under our charge, in many cases we have created a parent-child relationship with our team members. However, not only are we spoiling our adopted 'children,' but we are allowing their influence to decide our direction. We have falsely empowered people to believe that their emotions and feelings are more important than anything else. We have established that the wants and needs of the person(s) **take priority** over those of the business. Please note that I did not say emotions are not important, but we have in fact regressed to the point where individual feelings have taken priority over team health and performance.

For those who are committed to serving others emotionally or who need emotional attention or hand-holding, they might be better served working with a church, a global mission, or a non-profit. These are better options vs engaging with the focus and discipline required for organizational team health and survival. It is true that people build the business, but at the same time, people cannot exist if they don't have a business to build.

Benefits: None to the organization. Personal feelings are validated by the person. Especially dangerous when it's a leader.

Risks: Team division/splinter groups, halted progress, false objectives, diminished leadership, political outcomes, emotional influence creates a loss of control, and poor performance.

How to Address this: Rule out any possible valid, fact-based issues, vs personal feelings or opinions. Let people know their feelings are important but stick to the facts, don't feed ideals. Remind them that this is indeed a business and ask what they can do to help the team. Help them to shift their focus from themselves and their cause, onto the team mission. Don't apologize for claims made about feelings without logic or fact. For example, if someone says I feel like you are overlooking me for promotion because I am ____(fill in the spot), and the evidence clearly points to the fact that they aren't qualified for promotion due to lack of results or qualifications, don't say I'm sorry. Instead say, "Thank you for coming to me." Let's talk about:

- "Are you aware of the requirement for promotion?"
  - Gain acknowledgment: yes or no

  Then say,
- "Let's talk about what you haven't been doing," or
- "Let's talk about what you need to do, in order to be considered for a promotion."
- "Are you ok with that?"

Then start talking leadership philosophy, move into strategy, and finally ask them what they now know they need to do.

Cancel Culture – canceling is not, in fact, a valid culture. It is the product of emotionally broken people. Those who live in the cancel culture mindset believe that "What I feel is so real, that you must accept it as truth. If you don't, I have the power, along with others to take punitive action against you. I might try to remove you or your perspective that is making me 'feel' uncomfortable." They are insecure people who hide behind the cloak of social media to make the world righteous according to their standards. This is emotional inadequacy, which drives a radical and unbalanced behavior seeking to make the person feel better or feel in control. This behavior is also known as a temper tantrum or tantrum behavior.

According to Medlineplus.gov:

Temper tantrums are disruptive behaviors or emotional outbursts. They often occur in response to unmet needs or desires. Tantrums are more likely to occur in younger children or others who cannot express their needs or control their emotions when they are frustrated.

Benefits: None to the organization. Personal power is validated by the person by controlling the narrative and outcomes. This is especially dangerous when it's a leader.

Risks: Bullying environment created by the cancel culture (when/where does it stop), company potentially dissolving, team division/splinter groups, personal control, political outcomes, halted progress, diminished leadership, imbalance of power influence creates a political/personal cause vs a team mission.

How to Address this: Rule out any possible valid, fact-based issues over personal feelings or opinions. Let people know their feelings are important but stick to the facts, don't feed ideals. Remind them that this is indeed a business and ask what they can do to adjust, vs requiring someone or others to change or leave. Help them to shift their focus from themselves and their cause, onto the team mission. Don't apologize or give in to personal claims made about feelings without logic or fact.

For example, if someone says "You are _____, because I say so, (fill in the spot), and the evidence clearly points to the fact that this is not true, don't apologize for something that isn't true. Instead say,
- "Thank you for coming to me.
  Tell me what you are concerned about?"
  • Gain agreement if it is a concern: yes or no
  Then say,
- "Let's talk about what you can do to adjust," or
- "If the same situation applied to you, would you want us to do what you are asking us to do to this person?
- Help them to understand that it is ok not to like something, but it isn't ok to cancel something just because you don't like it.

Bias Culture – occurs when we have a bias (or prejudice) towards a certain group or an individual which creates an imbalance of interest. Most people think bias is strictly about favoring or un-favoring a certain group of minority people due to skin color, race, nationality, or gender. Bias is always wrong and must be addressed immediately when it is first noticed.

However, we must also be aware of reverse bias. This is when we favor the minority group or when we un-favor the majority group to lift-up the minority group. Bias is never acceptable. But neither is reverse bias. Our goal should be to seek balance, not a culture of "more than." More than takes away from one group and gives unfairly to the other group. Reverse bias creates an imbalance because we are merely filling an emotional need. Balance is always the key.

I once worked with a client who had a female leader that claimed the company had a biased, male-dominated culture. Although there was no evidence to support the claim, this female leader was adamant and on a mission. It was all opinion and emotion, creating a self-fulfilled problem. As a result, the female leader worked hard at running off or demoting many of the males in leadership roles that she felt threatened by. The result: The company now had a heavy female leadership, making the males the minority and insecure. Men were now claiming they were being treated with a bias, and they were right. She had created a culture of reverse bias.

Benefits: None to the organization. Personal power is validated by the person by controlling the narrative and outcomes. Especially dangerous when it's a leader.

Risks: Hostile work environment (when/where does it stop), company potentially getting sued, team division/splinter groups, personal or team control, radical outcomes, halted progress, diminished leadership, imbalance of power influence creates a public concern. False narratives/accusations created.

How to Address this: Rule out any possible valid, fact-based issues vs personal feelings or opinions. Ask people for evidence of their claims. Stick to the facts, don't feed opinions. Help them to shift their focus from themselves and their cause, onto the team mission. Don't apologize or give in to personal claims made without logic or fact. For example, if someone says "We are biased against _____, because we all feel that way, (fill in the spot), and the evidence clearly points to the fact that this is not true, then let them know.
Don't say I'm sorry. Instead say,
- "Thank you for coming to me, but what you are saying doesn't appear to align with what is really happening." Let's talk about it:
- "Can you give me valid instances of when, where, how, and who was involved?"
  - Gain agreement: yes or no

If no evidence, then say:
- "Let's talk about why you see things this way," or
- "If we made changes based on what you are asking, how would the changes affect the others on the team?"
- Help them to understand that a personal perspective doesn't translate into a wrong reality.
- If a leader is making these false claims, you should consider counseling them and watch their behavior closely.
- **Remember, just because a person is offended by something, that doesn't make it offensive.**

When we support these types of unhealthy cultural behaviors, as listed above, we have not only become part of the problem, we are now validating the new problem; we have forfeited being a leader. This is how the results appear:

High Culture/Low performance - meaning pleasing our people is the priority over our performance, and our results will be anemic long-term. This model is a major problem in HR heavy or people-pleasing organizations and creates people drag.

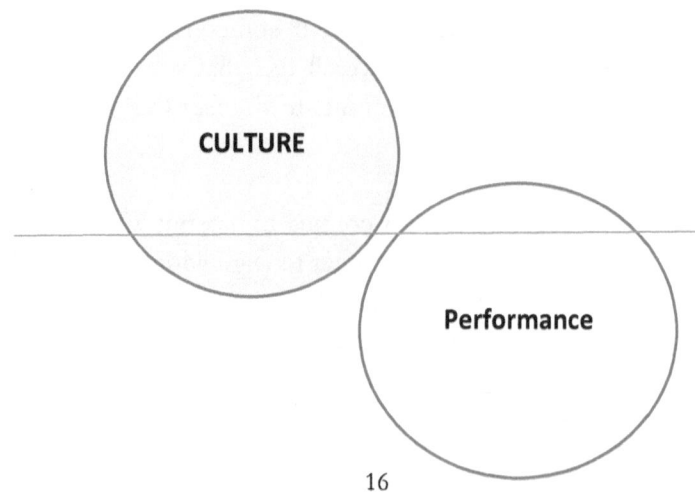

Chapter I – The Leadership System of 3

A few years ago, I was called on to advise a company that was experiencing a steady decline in performance. After a thorough investigation with many interviews, I determined the problem. I concluded that the leaders had created a high culture/low-performance environment. Culture-wise, the leadership team had consistently given-in to the requests and unreasonable demands of their people. They had good intentions, but made mistakes like putting out surveys asking, "How can we make you happy?" The team responded by asking for free lunches, more money, casual attire, work from home, no meetings, and whatever else they could think of to make them happy. The problem here wasn't the team, it was the leaders. In hopes of making everyone happy, the leaders complied and provided the perks requested. This created a high culture.

At the same time these new perks went into place, performance dropped. The reason why is that the message the team received was "Our happiness is the most important!" Since working towards accountability didn't make them happy. Had the leaders agreed to some of the terms and then clearly outlined the 'new expectations' of performance metrics associated with the perks at the same time, they would have experienced a different outcome. I helped them make adjustments and they immediately started to realize changes in two key areas:

1. **People left.** Interestingly enough, the people who left were the complainers who had capitalized on the high culture/low team performance. They were the major contributors of resistance by creating 'people drag.'

2. **Performance improved.** Those who stayed said that while they enjoyed the perks, they also noticed that many people had started slacking, and ironically, work wasn't fun anymore. Many stepped up and were soon promoted.

Performance

On the surface, the word performance sounds great. However, performance, like culture is a result of behavior. For example, a performance plan is a plan that promotes performance. The individual must perform, the plan does nothing. There are risks with being a heavy-driven, performance culture as well.

Performance-Heavy – Is a clear indicator that you have an inexperienced leader. When you remember that performance is an outcome, a performance-heavy environment places more emphasis on the result than the people, purpose, or the plan. Heavy tactics become the driver, which increases the risk of error or failure. Ironically, a performance heavy team might succeed briefly, but the model is not sustainable. Turnover or burnout is often the result. This is how the results appear:

Low Culture with high performance - means that performance is the priority over our people, and results are increased temporarily, but never for an extended period. Where a high culture, low-performance environment seeks to highly please the team, this environment seeks to highly please the leaders desired outcome. This also creates people drag.

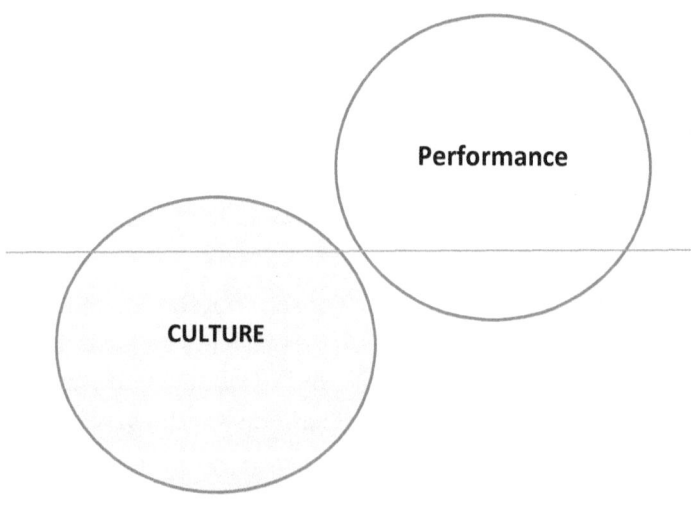

Balanced Team: Culture and Performance

When we are able to respect, develop, and support our people for the greater team mission, and they respond, train, and engage properly, we can realize the benefits of consistent results. This is called a balanced team. This is how the results appear: A focused Culture with focused Performance, meaning both our people and their performance are an equal priority.

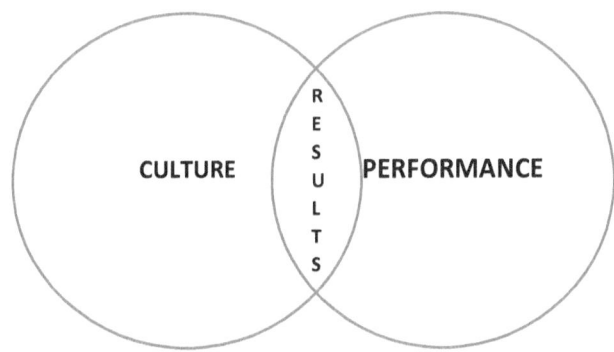

When considering how you impact or influence your own culture and performance, I'm sure you can figure out that results start with the behavioral approach of the leader. Remember, **it is either fashionable to perform or it is acceptable not to.**

BALANCED vs UNBALANCED LEADERS

The Unbalanced Leader – The System of 2

Like most leaders, Sandy was unbalanced. She was intent on running things her own way and worked hard to let everyone know she was in charge. Sure, she was nice at times, but her lack of leadership expertise was starting to show. Sandy lacked vision, strategic thinking, and she avoided receiving feedback. Ironically, Sandy believed she was acting in the best interest of everyone.

Chapter I – The Leadership System of 3

As the company approached the end of another quarter, Sandy was frustrated. Her team had once again missed the established performance metrics, and because she was an unbalanced leader, her emotions were taking over her logic. This caused her to use **a system of 2: Her viewpoint, fueled by emotions, caused her to go straight to action (tactics).**

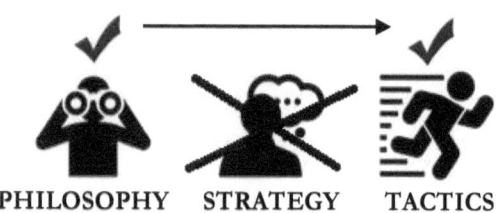

PHILOSOPHY   STRATEGY   TACTICS

Sandy was 'strategically' anemic. She lived in a tactical mindset, driven by a broken philosophy. Her vision was only on her point of view and her desired outcome. When things weren't up to Sandy's standards, her philosophy caused her to jump straight to tactics, **avoiding strategy**. This caused her to avoid critical strategic planning and rendered her results ineffective. This prompted her to say things like, "we need **to do more**, we need **to hire better** people, we need **to change things**." Yes, change needed to happen, but not in the way Sandy wanted; Sandy needed to change her unbalanced approach.

For those paying attention, the driving component to Sandy's leadership was always "do." This is called a 'tactical approach' and is common among most untrained leaders today. The tactical approach causes leaders and their teams to become unbalanced. Since unbalanced leaders lack proper philosophy, they fail to strategize, causing them to live in the ineffective world of "We NEED TO DO." Unbalanced leaders are 'action-centric.' When teams keep 'doing the same things,' or worse, doing 'more' of the 'wrong things,' without strategizing 'why, what, or how' they are doing things, they will continue to fail.

The Balanced Leader – The System of 3

As a leader, it's not about what you do. It's about how you 'view' what you strategically plan to do, how you 'think about and plan' to do what you thought about, and how well you 'execute' on your strategic plan.

For the Lion Leader, all three of these components must be present. They must be a product of each other, and they must produce continuity and consistency by working together. I call this "The System of 3"

THE SYSTEM OF 3

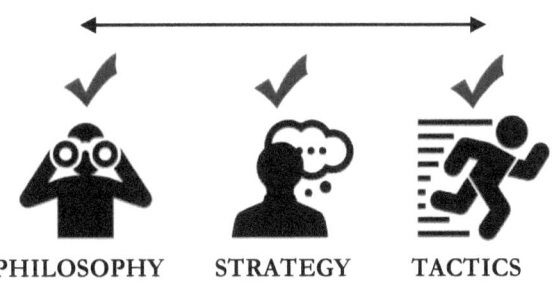

PHILOSOPHY   STRATEGY   TACTICS

1. Philosophy is a viewpoint or thought only. It's the first critical phase of anything you do. **Philosophy by my definition is: HOW YOU VIEW or think about what you are doing or what you are going to do.**

Most leaders never evaluate their philosophy. They don't honestly ask questions like, how do I view my work, my people, my role, my mission, my outcomes, and my purpose? Why am I even doing this job? Most merely get a job for the paycheck or worse, for the title. That is an unsustainable personal philosophy. These people merely hope for the best, relying primarily on lessons from their past to push them through. What these leaders fail to understand is that this approach is in fact a philosophy, but a personal one. It is a philosophy of complacency supported by a strategy of "hope for the best," for me.

Your philosophy is the foundational element to success in every endeavor in your life. If you don't have a positive or healthy viewpoint about what you are doing, you are most certainly destined to fail, or you will merely skate by until you fail. Please know my intent isn't to be negative, this is a fundamental truth. Here is why:

How you view things, affects how you plan to do them. Therefore, when you view something poorly or for the wrong reasons, you will plan improperly or not at all. As an example, if you view yourself as an inadequate leader, you probably won't plan (strategize) or think about ways to become a better leader, therefore, you will not execute well (tactics). Your flawed philosophy will cause you to generate flawed results. This is problematic and can become circular.

- The more you think the wrong thoughts, then...
- the less action or wrong actions you will take, then...
- you will get poor results, which will cause you to
- think the wrong thoughts...
- starting the cycle over and over.

Solution: Work with a mentor or an established Lion Leader you trust who has your best interest in mind. Review with your mentor how you think about your current life and career: your role, your company, etc., and ask them to help you identify areas where you have been focused negatively or on the wrong things. Seek to understand why you think the wrong way and then commit to see things differently but be honest. For example, if you view your work as a burden, identify what items you see as a burden, then evaluate why.
- Is it really a burden, or do you just dislike certain tasks?
- What do you dislike about the tasks?
- Are the tasks required?

- How can you view the tasks differently?
- Ask: Am I willing to change how I view things?
- Remember, you don't have to like everything you do, but if the tasks are required, as a matter of integrity, you must do them.

2. Strategy is the active, measurable, and detailed planning phase only. It is the second critical phase (and most neglected) of anything you do. **Strategy by my definition is: How you PLAN TO DO what you have been doing or have been thinking about doing.**

Remember, how you view it (philosophy) affects how you plan to do it (strategy). Most leaders never evaluate their philosophy, so they certainly don't strategize effectively on how to do it or they skip the strategy and go straight to tactics. Also, many leaders often confuse strategy with tactics (our next topic). For clarification, remember that strategy happens from the neck up. I often say that when people who have strategy without action, have BIG HEADS!

Strategy is the cognitive part of The System of 3. Strategy involves deliberate and thoughtful planning only. While philosophy influences strategy, action is not present in strategy.

Solution: This requires a team approach. You don't know it all and therefore you must gather input from the expertise and insight of your team. Talk as a team about:
- What you have been doing and what you have not been doing (tactics).
- What is working and what isn't.
- What are other options?
- What are you missing that you need?

- What are the current risks or liabilities?
- Who else needs to be involved?
- What other resources do you need?
- What skills need to be developed?
- What can you modify, change, or stop doing?
- Should we even be doing this??

3. Tactics are the active, measurable, and detailed actions only. Tactics happen from the neck down.
They are the third critical phase (and most overused) of anything you do. **Tactics by my definition: How you actually DO what you have been thinking about and planning.**

How you view what you are doing (philosophy) affects how you plan to do it (strategy), and therefore ultimately drives what you do (tactics), impacting your results. I often say that people who take action without strategizing have BIG FEET! Our research has shown that when most leaders and teams are faced with a problem or poor performance, they usually jump directly to phase 3 (Tactics) to make course corrections. This is chronic within organizations and you can notice it by simply listening to others when problems arise. When people operate primarily from a tactical perspective, they will jump straight to the tactical phase, using tactical verbiage. I call this flawed tactic the **'Do More' Approach.** You might hear something like this:
- **We <u>need to make</u> more calls**
- **We <u>need to set</u> more meetings**
- **You <u>need to do</u> more reports, or**
- **We <u>need to 'do more'</u> of whatever it is that the emotional, unbalanced leader deems necessary.**

Remember, if you have a flawed philosophy or strategy, **'doing more'** of the same 'wrong' isn't going to get you right results or even better results. Instead, I challenge leaders to utilize The System of 3 completely, as a circular phase. This means that when you get the wrong results, instead of staying in the tactical phase of 'DO MORE,' you move back to philosophy. You stay in this stage until you align purposefully, then you move to strategy to plan again as a team. Finally, after your new strategy has been agreed on, THEN you move to tactics to take your new actions. We can call this new approach the:

- **See More (broader, deeper philosophy),**
- **Know More (strategize effectively), and**
- **DO Better approach (execute tactically better).**

Solution: When you aren't getting the results you desire, there is always a valid reason and simply 'doing more' is the easy way out for the inexperienced leader. Your deficiency might be something simple enough that you are missing, but you must go through all phases of the system of 3 to address your issues. You always start with your philosophy.

1. **Evaluate** not only your personal philosophy but also the philosophy of your team. How do they view the work they are doing? As an example, if they view their work poorly, you will get poor results.
2. **Recommit** as a group to strategize together and design a new plan to approach your deficiency with purpose. You must address the flawed philosophy as well.
3. **Take new or better actions**, but this time, measure, get feedback, gain new information, and evaluate on a weekly basis to catch issues before they get out of control.

Chapter I – The Leadership System of 3

The System of 3 approach can effectively address the chronic problem with most leaders today. We are tactically driven. This means we tend to incorrectly focus more on the actions our people take:
- what our people are doing, that they shouldn't be,
  or
- what they aren't doing, that they should be.

Instead of seeking to understand why and how they do it. We lack strategy because we lack true vision and purpose. The System of 3 approach requires more effort, time, and dedication from the leader while developing or realigning your purpose.

When people cannot see the vision of the plan, they will not follow the plan.

Chapter I – The Leadership System of 3

What is YOUR Leadership Philosophy?

How do I view leadership?

_____

_____

How do I view my role as a leader?

_____

_____

Why do I view it that way?

_____

_____

What can I alter or adjust to improve how I view leadership?

_____

_____

Chapter II – The Power of Strategy

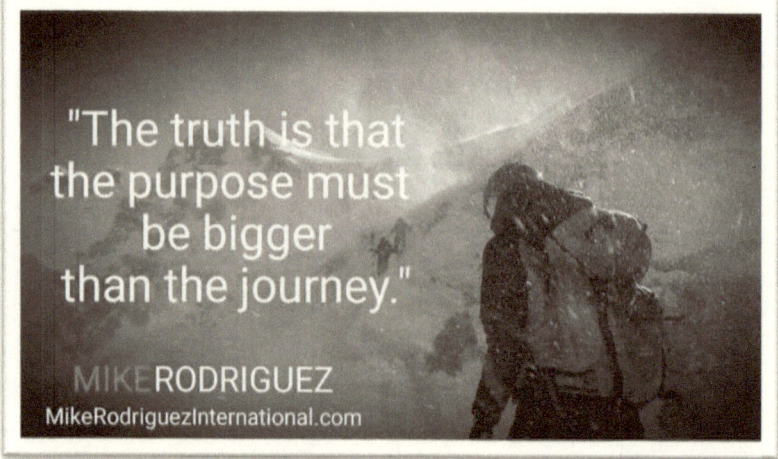

> "Tactics without strategy
> is the noise before defeat."
>
> Sun Tzu

II

The POWER of Strategy

When you consider that 92% of leaders lack professional leadership training, we can easily conclude that leaders are not effectively strategizing on the actions that are being taken. This means that they aren't putting detailed, vetted thought into their evaluation, insight, and review by utilizing the System of 3. When surveyed, most leaders indicate that they formulate or emulate their leadership style:
- from others,

or
- from previously learned experiences with past leaders they worked for or with.

As a result, we aren't seeing new growth or critical strategic thinking, rather we are seeing chronic examples of a non-strategic, copy-cat culture of leaders. We have categorized these as follows:

STRATEGIC CATEGORIES
No Strategy (Emotional Driver, Logical Fallacy)

You might think that this is impossible, but people, especially inexperienced leaders, do this daily. Corporate teams (sales, HR, marketing, etc.) operate without strategy frequently, although they would never acknowledge it. If you have ever taken an action with thinking it through, only focusing on the end results, you were operating without strategy; or if you have ever not taken an action because you weren't willing to think it through (you are always able), then you were operating without strategy.

During a recent executive coaching call, my client stated that he was concerned about the lack of results of his sales teams. When I asked him what the problem was, he said that sales had dropped considerably. He immediately started talking about how they needed to make more calls and set more new meetings. When I asked him about their sales techniques and processes, he said his team was very experienced with vast sales skills. Not only was this not answering my questions, but he revealed much more to me; he wasn't aware of his team's deficiencies; therefore, he could not be using a strategic plan. He was in arrogant denial, relying on false hope. He was hoping that because the team was 'experienced,' meaning they had been in sales for a period of time, that the experience miraculously translated into success. My friends, this isn't strategy, this is an example of the absence of strategy or 'No Strategy.' It is in fact the presence of an emotional driver, backed by logical fallacy. Just because someone is experienced, doesn't mean they can or will succeed. In addition, an experienced person will know their strategic approach, which has been crafted from their past failures.

Low Strategy (Emotional Pull, Logical Hope)

When I was a senior in high school, two friends and I concocted a brilliant idea for spring break. All of us were broke (no jobs), but we did have access to a car that often broke down, burned oil, and was one trip away from the junkyard.

One night while we were emotionally charged, we convinced ourselves that we had all the resources we needed to drive the 500+ miles to the beach in Texas. We decided that if we bought a case of oil, we could keep filling up the engine, and if we each borrowed fifty dollars, we could cover the cost of gas and food. In addition, we were convinced that the accommodations would be covered by my sister who lived in Port Arthur. Our reasoning, surely my sister would welcome me and my rebel friends once we showed up uninvited after driving for over eight hours. To us, our idea was solid!

As you can imagine that plan failed miserably because it wasn't strategic. It was an emotionally-driven idea, validated with a logical fallacy, by emotional people. Emotions work that way; they can be powerful drivers. They can convince us that even though nothing really makes sense that our desire to 'want to succeed' can deceive us into believing things make sense 'to us.'

When you believe in something emotionally and jump into it without effective, logical strategic planning, you are destined to fail. **This is called an Emotional Pull.** The Emotional Pull is highly active in business today. Some people within companies are giving advice on matters that they know nothing about. Some leaders are making emotional decisions all in the name of truth and love, where truth doesn't exist, and love is really translated into 'pleasing the crowd.' This isn't leadership; it is ineffective people-pleasing. It is equivalent to the decision my young friends and I made to travel to the beach in the scenario above. We were destined to fail, and we did. If you are making decisions the same way, then you too will meet the same fate that we did: complete failure.

Sometimes though emotions can't be avoided. When they are heavily present, we must still go through due diligence to offset and mitigate risks. We must execute as efficiently as possible. Here is another more relevant scenario:

In early 2020 a pandemic had propagated globally, affecting just about every person and organization in operation. As of the writing of this book, hundreds of thousands of businesses have shut down, but that is only the result of the problem. Thousands of leaders have taken wrong action after wrong action, all in the name of doing the right thing. But what is the right thing? Who determines it? And how was it determined to begin with?

In many cases, we are seeing leaders who are making reactive, tactical decisions without having a fact-based, strategic understanding of what they are doing. The evidence is clearly displayed as most are executing poorly and the results show it. In most instances, leaders have jumped straight into a tactical approach fueled by a philosophy of emotion. They are possibly convicted about their incorrect actions, fed by their incorrect thoughts and emotional team input, without truly understanding why or what they are doing. When your results contrast greatly with the original goal, we can know with certainty that your execution has failed. When execution fails, we must always revert

to and evaluate our original purpose and strategy to ensure that we are aligned properly as a team:
- with our vision,
- with our strategic plans
- with the outcome we established and expect.

Low strategy happens when we are influenced by emotion, but we still work at doing something, although the core of the message is high emotion and limited data without complete logic. For example, your team might say "We need our business to survive, so we will do what everyone else is doing in order to be looked at favorably by the market." When you hope that an approach works, based on the unvetted variables you put into place, you are working with low strategy and logical hope. It's no different than finding a broken rope bridge across a stream you want to cross, pushing a fallen log across, and simply hoping it all works out. There is a chance you might succeed, but a greater risk that you will fail. In life as in business, you must work to mitigate risks in order to avoid the fall.

GO! Strategy (Logical Pull, Emotional Push)

The most efficient model involves building a strategy with minimal risk assessed while using your emotional drivers to engage your strategy. This model doesn't mean you won't fail, but it means you will prepare adequately and logically. The difference here is that the emotions aren't the basis of the action, they are the fuel behind the action. In my previous story, had my friends and I used this model, we would have succeeded. We would have worked through logical details, asked an adult with reliable transportation to drive us, called my sister and gained approval, and possibly worked jobs to earn money. Our emotions would have pushed us to engage in those healthy tasks, not derail us. Strategizing would have created a better outcome. As it would have created a greater chance of success for our trip.

What about you and your teams?

- Do you tend to be reactive?
- Do you let emotions drive your thoughts, words, and actions?
- Do you often act with little strategic planning?
- Do you have ideas, but neglect to vet them, taking action and simply hoping for the best?

If you said yes to any of these, you need to slow down and engage properly with your team. Start with everyone's mindset.

THE 3 MINDSETS

Your mindset and the mindset of those on your team is critical to if and how, you strategically plan, and if and how, you take action. My research has concluded that there are three core types of mindsets that people tend to operate within life and in the workplace. These mindsets are the drivers of personal philosophy and create a direct impact on performance.

Chapter II – The Power of Strategy

1. The Complainers – Create Resistance

This group makes up about 20% of people, yet they create the greatest damage to the overall health and direction of your organization. They are emotional thinkers. Complainers are not bad people they are merely focused on the wrong things. Their bad attitudes and low to no performance not only jeopardize their careers, but they also create negative effects on the organization.

Complainers show up to work (and life) because they are required to, meaning they need a paycheck. Something has happened in their lives that has prompted them to lose their focus, their passion, and their drive and since they work for you, you receive the product of their mindset. They aren't happy with some facet of their life, (it might be their job) and they let everyone know, either verbally or through their lack of engagement. These people are disappointing in many ways, but primarily because they show up to work, expecting 100% of their paycheck every pay period while refusing to give 100% effort in return. The core of their foundation is that they don't believe that much is happening or will happen in their lives, but they believe that they are owed much. Ironically, they create their own demise through self-destructive behavior.

Complainers are highly deficient in personal accountability and detrimental to the overall health of the organization. They come to work late, gossip, conduct personal tasks during business hours, have extended lunch hours, and they leave work early. Nothing is ever their fault, and they typically lead a life of blame and deflecting (it's not me, it's you). Most company cultures are impacted heavily by the complainers, especially when they see more and more complainers develop within the organization.

If you have ever worked at a company where people were telling you all the bad things about the employer, the people, product, and everything else they could find wrong, then you were working with complainers. Their disease is highly contagious, and their behavior should be addressed quickly with decisive action. Complainers are culture changers, negative impactors, and creators of resistance. Their poor attitudes not only affect their overall performance, but they will also hold back the progress of the entire team if you aren't a Lion Leader.

As a leader, your goal isn't to terminate the complainer; the goal is to get them to recognize their unacceptable behavior and to give them the opportunity to take immediate and planned action to correct it. Remember, any manager can fire someone, but a Lion Leader accepts every challenge to develop all employees and turn them around. Again, if any employee isn't willing to improve, then they have already made their decision. A Lion Leader learns this quickly and acts on it. When this happens, you must help the person to exit your organization with a legal, ethical, and soundproof plan. You do this for their own happiness and the health and culture of your organization.

The good news is that most complainers are indeed aware that they are complainers. They are normally not called out for their behavior, especially in today's market. So, when they are confronted, they will usually respond by either:

a. **getting back on board to win, or**
b. **resisting and planning their exit strategy.**

Either way is a win-win for both of you, but ultimately your goal is to get them to move up to the next level of performance and accountability or to move out. I have seen many chronic complainers stay with organizations for years because they are never called out for their behavior (poor leadership). I have seen many leave the organization and take their poor behavior somewhere else. Finally, I have seen a few complainers in my career who take responsibility for their actions, and they take action to improve (Lion Leadership). This group will always need the guidance and mentorship of a fair, caring, and true Lion Leader. One who doesn't negotiate with mediocrity.

2. The Complacent – The Sustainers

This group accounts for approximately 70% of people. Complacent people are the ones who show up and do their job. They are practical thinkers. They usually won't do any more, unless asked. These are the typical people who have fallen into the comfort of the daily routines of their lives. They have confused the fact that because they are doing something, and they are getting a result, that everything is fine. They live and operate from a perspective that as long as they are comfortable, all is okay. This simply isn't true, because when most complacent people increase their attitudes and action; we find that they can (and usually do) achieve more out of work and life.

The problem is that people in this group are comfortable and they don't want to get uncomfortable, which happens to be a requirement for change. They are capable of producing much more if they can only find a profound reason to take action. They are missing out on a much better quality of life, and they aren't giving the company the best that either of them deserves. Complacent people should be encouraged and challenged to become all that they are capable of. Lion Leaders help them find their reason to excel and help them grow to the next level.

3. The Competitors – The Performers

This third group is unique and accounts for less than 10% of people within an organization, but ironically, they have the greatest impact on the culture. They are strategic thinkers, blending emotion (as fuel) with logic to execute well. I have found that almost every person in this group has been a complainer or has been complacent at some point in their life or career. Competitors have experienced the same pains, failures, and personal challenges, yet what makes this group different is that they have decided to overcome these common obstacles to achieve something greater. The key here is a personal decision. **They have decided to show up and win.**

Competitors don't compete with others, rather they have decided to make changes to become the best person 'they' can be. Yes, people can change, but only when they are truly willing, and only when they make a commitment for themselves to change. As Lion leaders, we aren't called to change people, we are called to help them see that they can indeed change. We must help them to open their minds and believe.

Competitors have taken personal responsibility and therefore have taken action to make their lives better. They understand that by being a better employee, the organization and the people they work with become better as well. They understand that everyone benefits. Competitors show up to win, and they want others to win. They also recognize that winning is a decision. They have a purpose, they see the company vision, and they take accountability. They have developed the core qualities to become a Lion Leader, and you will find your leadership candidates in this group. However, know that there are two types of competitors:

Reckless Competitor
 These individuals are driven, but they are all about themselves. They will usually do or say whatever is necessary to get the end result to succeed, sometimes at any cost. People in this group won't usually be part of the team, but they can and sometimes do make the transition to become a

Balanced Competitor
 These are people who operate with integrity, passion, teamwork, strategy, and vision for the greater cause. They see the big picture and follow a plan to win. This is the category you should be promoting from.

Chapter II – The Power of Strategy

Competitors don't seek to compete with others. They have a bigger purpose and a greater vision. As a result, they seek to compete with themselves to become their best.

The Team Impact Snapshot:

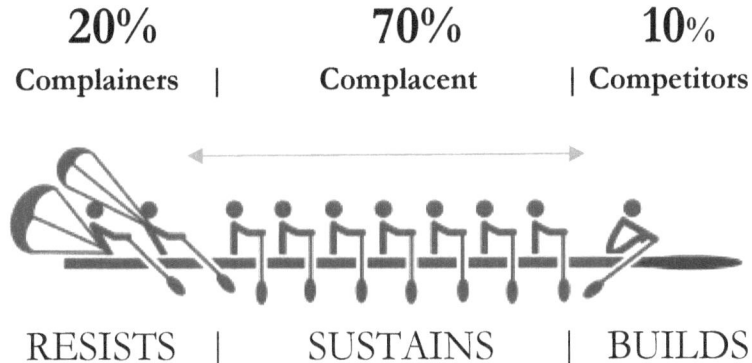

20%   **70%**   **10%**
Complainers | Complacent | Competitors

RESISTS | SUSTAINS | BUILDS

Team Impact Snapshot Summary
In a team with 70 people, these numbers translate into the performance of your people as follows:

- ✓ **14** people on your team are disengaged and creating degrees of resistance, preventing progress.
- ✓ **49** people on your team are engaged but are only sustaining your current progress made.
- ✓ **7** people on your team (including you) are focused, have a purpose, and are working towards more progress.

This is not Psychology, this is data.

When you factor in that your team is all in the same boat together, then you can see from the **Team Impact Snapshot** how each mindset (or groups of mindsets) is impacting your business. Consider these facts when evaluating your people:

- Not only do complainers hold themselves back, but they also hold back your entire team.
- Complainers actively recruit, so the lowest complacent are susceptible to being recruited by the complainers.
- Mindsets can and will adjust daily, move left and right as people encounter ever-changing daily events.
- If you don't lead your people well, the resistance will spread, and your business will start to fail.
- If your team gets to about 35% complainers, your business performance will cease.
- Your goal is to help every person get focused and engaged and to stay at the competitor level.
- **Setting the right expectations can course correct a flawed mindset.**

YES! People can change! (But you cannot change them.)

This is great news! Regardless of where you are as a leader, or where members of your team may be in any of these three categories, know that anyone can change if they choose to. They just need to come to their own realization of their mindset, recognize that they can change, and believe that you will support them. They need to know they are part of the team and part of the vision. This doesn't mean you compromise and lighten up on accountability, it means you challenge them to grow.

The decision to become a competitor is a living process. You will see each member of your team go through different stages. They will fall into and move out of each of the three categories based on their attitudes. Your job as a Lion Leader is to stay engaged and set the right expectations. When people see that you have their best interest at heart, that you believe in them, and that you have high expectations for them, they can surprise you with critical change. This doesn't require handholding; this requires setting new standards, then personally committing to attain them together.

STRATEGIC (COGNITIVE) THINKING

Leon Seltzer, PhD/Psychologist, states that "One of the most baffling problems is to acutely *feel* the reality of something without having any basis in fact." You must know that I am not a fan of Psychology because it is not a medical science, but it is in fact a pseudo-science; a creation from the mind of Sigmund Freud. However, I can still say that this statement should resonate with every leader as truth, so let's review a few facts:
- 86% of teams spend less than an hour a month on strategy.
- 90% of teams fail to execute strategies successfully.
- 83% of companies lack a contingency plan for difficulties.
- Teams who think strategically together attain greater success together!

(Sources: BDC, Forbes, Harvard Business, MRI)

The reason most people engage in the problem of acutely feeling the reality of things without having a basis, in fact, is because most people are emotional thinkers.

I recently watched a documentary on the effects of the 2011 Tohoku tsunami off the Pacific coast in Japan. The tsunami was devasting and destroyed many of the villages in the area. Afterward, many villages took initiative to rebuild without waiting on government assistance. As I watched, a city board sat in a meeting strategizing about how to move forward. They were deciding if they should still host their annual cultural celebration parade that had been held every year for hundreds of years.

As they strategized, many shared logical and positive input. One person said that they needed to host the parade to show progress for the village. Another said that it would allow the community to come together and show their resilience. But a third person spoke and said, "I don't agree... there are still many people who are grieving, and I feel they might not want to participate or celebrate." The room went quiet, but not in the way you think. The board disagreed with her (as they should have) and took a vote to move forward against her opinion.

This lady had good intentions, but ironically, she was creating resistance for all in the name of her personal emotions. She did not have data on who did or did not want to participate and therefore her opinion was not a relevant factor. In addition, they were all committed to moving forward, except for her.

It was obvious that the entire village had experienced devastation, but it was also obvious that they needed to move forward. Yes, people had died, but there were two points to factor in:

1. Those families who had experienced loss were grieving and had the right to decide on their own if they wanted to take part in the celebration.
2. What about those families who wanted to move on? Should they be forced to miss out because this one woman felt that SOME needed to grieve, therefore ALL should?

This emotional board member was exhibiting Inside-In thinking: opinion based and all hypothetical thought. Since this event happened in a different culture, they respected the lady's opinion but held out on their broader culture over personal opinions. However, in the U.S. we are more inclined to give in to emotionally-driven thinking over the broader picture for all. This is problematic for society in general, but also for organizations. When we allow the opinions of a few control the greater cause for all, there is a great risk and a greater cost. We hold everyone back and start to decline.

Just because 'one' person thinks, feels, or believes it, doesn't make it true for 'all.'

Chapter II – The Power of Strategy

"Inside-IN" Emotional Thinking - is when we receive or accept information or a thought into our minds (input). Then we seek to resolve or reconcile that input on our own, with our personal, emotional perspective.

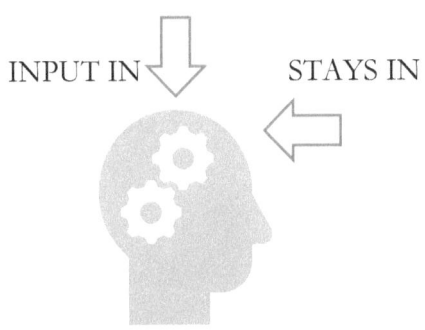

INPUT IN   STAYS IN

MAKES US DEPENDENT ON OURSELVES

This happens because the thinker lacks or avoids the basis of the facts, adding personal truth. In some instances, the Inside-In thinker takes their position to other people. They do this to seek validation about the thoughts and emotions **they have already reconciled within themselves**.

The Inside-In thinker might seek social, team, or public validation, so they, and everyone else, can accept their emotional input 'as truth' or 'fact.' Once they have social acceptance, they can feel empowered about their false belief to apply it to everyone. This can also be called Confirmation Bias: where the thinker only seeks out the information necessary to validate or confirm their position, belief, or bias. The risk with Inside-In Thinking is that it keeps us bound emotionally to our thoughts, making us dependent on ourselves. This type of thinking lacks emotional maturity and prevents growth for everyone. In a team environment, Inside-In thinking causes leaders to be followers, and followers to take control. **Lion Leaders challenge popular opinion when popular opinion is wrong. They do what is right, not what is popular.**

Chapter II – The Power of Strategy

"Inside-OUT" Logical Thinking - is when we receive information or a thought into our minds (input). However, instead of personal reconciliation like the Inside-In thinker, The Inside-Out thinker **seeks external data and truth for reconciliation.** That source might be with the team, through research, or even by talking with someone with experience who can tell you what you need to hear, not just what you want to hear. This is also cognitive thinking by conscious intellectual thought.

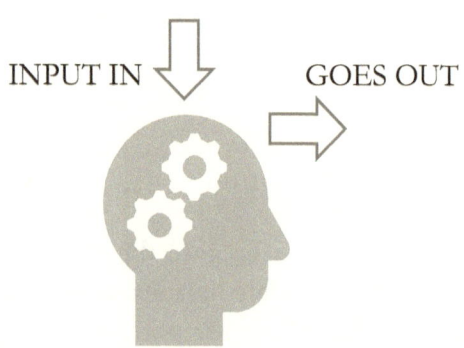

HELPS US COMMIT TO THE MISSION

When we choose to seek the truth, gain facts, do research, and vet our feelings, we can gain new information. When we gain new, fact-based information, we can now make new, logical decisions. This can help us change our direction and outcome to support the greater cause.

Emotional thinking puts you in the passenger seat. Logical thinking puts you in the driver's seat. It demands that you take new logical steps for the betterment of all, not just to fulfill your personal agenda.

To become a strategic thinker, it is important to have an awareness of the connection between your mind and your mouth. Your brain is the central processing system of your body, your mouth is merely flesh and bone that pushes out and forms words with your tongue and air from your lungs. Think about that for a minute. What you say is truly a reflection of your thoughts. With that, one of the key tips for strategic thinking is: **Don't talk about what you can't do, focus on what you can do and get it done.**

When you take this reasonable, action-based approach, you are exercising logical, "Inside-OUT" thinking. In addition, you are setting an example for your team. As a leader, you are helping to establish your culture. With that, you either have an:

Emotional Culture: Driven by personal opinions or bias
Example:
- I feel
- I think
- I believe
- Seems like
- Looks like
- For me...
- It must be true
- I hope

or

Cognitive Culture: Driven by strategic thought and facts.
Example: Since "A" is factually causing "B," therefore we need to "C."

When evaluating your culture and making the shift to cognitive thinking, you must understand the key steps to become a cognitive culture. You do this by asking questions. The most neglected question with any team when facing a challenge is **"What is our top priority?"** When you ask this question, you shift the team focus from opinions to logical outcomes.

Emotions are indeed important, but they should never be a factor over facts, data, and logic for life and business decisions.

Here are the steps you can follow to keep your culture cognitive:

1. **Discuss your team priority** – welcome and evaluate factual input only.
2. **Gain Agreement** – It's ok not to understand the team priority, but it's not ok to be resistant for personal or emotional reasons.
3. **Build around the priority** – Send out a communication, recap in meetings, and hold each other accountable.
4. **Finally, consistently ask each other when matters come up - Does this align with 'our priority?'**

You'll find that this strategic approach keeps everyone aligned with the team mission and vets out personal agendas or matters that seek to derail your culture.

Strategic thinking is *more* than just thinking outside the box.
It's knowing *which* box to think outside of!

COGNITIVE PREPARATION

It's easy to bring people together for strategic planning. It is considerably more difficult to choose to work together. You must realize that in order to truly collaborate, you must be willing to think together strategically. The problem here is that most people are too focused on themselves.

Illuminate Your Own Lightbulb (The HMMM Factor)

You can drive yourself crazy trying to convince someone to be aware of or recognize a problem, especially when it is their own problem. The most effective method is called self-illumination or allowing someone to illuminate their own lightbulb. You could tell them the problem (make a statement):

- **"You had a low performance last month."**

After hearing your words, they would probably disagree or try to figure out where you were coming from. A better option would be for you to ask them a question that would prompt them to cognitively engage and think about your question (hmmm?). For example, you might now ask:

- **"Were you aware of your performance results last month?"**

Their only options are: YES or NO. If they say YES, then you are in agreement and you can continue talking.

If they say NO, then you would promptly provide them with the data validating their low performance last month. You would then ask them if they are aware now, once they have the data, and then you would be in agreement. You could now start strategizing the new tactical actions to take together.

The Key 3 for Cognitive Preparation:

1. **Gather Facts**
   What are the matters related to the success or failure of the project or mission? In other words, saying "I don't think this will work" is not acceptable.
2. **Evaluate Data**
   What has happened in the past? What data do we have that supports our claims or actions? What is the data we have to help us decide?
3. **Measure Results**
   What are the numbers and measurable metrics that we need to look at?

Remember, numbers don't lie, people do.

Cognitive Killers: are the products from the mind of the emotional person. They might come across as sincere or even genuine, but you must separate them from the facts:

- **Personal opinions** (or personal agenda)
  Information without facts or data that might seek to serve the person giving them.
- **Negative feelings**
  Content shared in a manner that reflects personal resistance, emotion, or a bias in content or delivery.
- **Conscious bias**
  Behavior that is demonstrated intentionally against someone. (There is no such thing as unconscious or subconscious bias.) You cannot get into someone's mind to see if they have a bias. People consciously know when they have a bias.
- **Emotional reactions**
  I have witnessed people without facts, who have yelled in meetings, through tears, that they are right. In every instance, they were wrong.

Data Steps - How to use Data as a Team:
D – Decide what is needed together
A – Anticipate the possible risks and challenges
T – Think outside of the right boxes
A – Agree on closure and alignment

Make Adjustments
1. **Avoid conflict: Seek the Balance Point.**
   The point that lies between emotion and logic is reason. We call this the balance point. As we have determined, most people live in the mindset of **emotion.** Others live in the contrasting mindset of pure logic. The balance point allows you to understand the emotional perspective, but to neutralize it by introducing logic into the conversation.

For example, if you bring in a direct report for counseling and the direct report responds emotionally, saying: "I feel like you don't like me." You can respond like this: "That isn't true, I do like you, however, that isn't the issue. This conversation is about your low performance of 55% over the last two months. Your low performance is what I don't like." You can then follow up by asking: "Can you understand how 55% is not acceptable?"

In this scenario, you have acknowledged the emotional component without feeding it and you introduced logic into the conversation. Now you have brought the conversation to the balance point of reason.

Seek the Balance Point

Emotion ⟹ **REASON** ⟸ Logic

Never argue to prove you are right...
Talk to work towards a resolution.

2. **Avoid Logical Fallacy**
Logical fallacy speaks to our errors in our reasoning that invalidate our argument. Emotional people like to validate what they are saying, so do logical people. Either way, we must make sure that when we are seeking a resolution and we aren't giving in to unreasonable validation. Here is an example of a logical fallacy: **All tigers are striped, some domestic cats are striped, therefore some domestic cats are tigers.** On the surface, this appears logical, but it is in fact idiotic because it is unreasonable. Here is an example of

logical fallacy presented in the workplace that is very common today: **Because I drastically feel that we have a bias in our company, others must feel this is a problem, therefore everyone must take drastic steps to correct the problem.**

Make sure that you don't let dominant or overzealous emotional people drive a wedge into your culture. You'll do this every time you believe their logical fallacy and then sell others their fallacy as truth.

3. **Think "TEAM" not "ME"**

   I know that you are probably thinking that this is so cliché. But the truth is that in today's world, most of your people are ME-centric, not WE-centric. The challenge here is that a ME-centric person will always create resistance (think Complainer). **In fact, resistance is the tactic usually employed by those whose ideas are inferior to others.**
   Instead, get your people to move from:
   Personal expectation:

   "I want"
   TO
   ⬇
   TEAM Standard: "We Need"

Examples:
Personal Expectation: "I'm so frustrated, I really want everyone on the team to respond to my emails faster.
Team Standard: "In order for us to be more efficient, we need everyone to start responding to emails with 24 hours."

4. **Expect Success!**
   It might sound simple enough, but most people do not expect success, they merely hope that somehow, things will just happen! When a pride of lions gets up to hunt, they don't hope things work out. Their survival is at stake, so they expect success. When you commit to becoming a strategic thinker, you elevate your confidence and create a cognitive culture of people who:
   1. **Know your top priorities as a team**
   2. **Use the right resources**
   3. **Make adjustments as a team, and therefore....**
   4. **EXPECT SUCCESS!**

Remember, you will always encounter failure; failure is an equal and necessary part of success. But strategic thinkers keeping going until they find a new way!

STRATEGIC (ACTIVE) LISTENING:
Listening Facts

Of all the life and business skills, while communication is by far the most important, active listening is easily the most neglected. When you factor in the data you can see that listening is the most critical communication skill:
- 85% of what we learn is through listening, not talking
- 75% of the time we are preoccupied or forgetful
- We listen at 125-250 WPM, but 'think' at 1k-3k WPM
- Less than 2% of the population has formal listening training

(Shorpe, Hunsaker, HighGain, Inc.)

Understand Active Listening

Dr. Ralph G. Nichols, who fathered the study and development of the field of listening, states that, "The most basic of all human needs is the need to understand and be understood. The best way to understand people is to listen to them."

This seems simple enough, but like most basic concepts, ironically this concept is one of the most neglected. To better position ourselves as leaders who are active listeners, we must understand that the foundation of active listening is born from how we view people. How we view people is typically an indicator of how we treat them. There are two key views on how we view the people we communicate with:

- **Functional** - people are merely a required part of the communication process,
- **Relational** - we are concerned not only with how we communicate but also with how we connect with people.

Our core goal in effective communication is to build the kind of aural (of the ears) experience that uses the skill of active listening. We do this to build relational connections. **Wait!......Did I just write that Active Listening is a skill? Yes, I did!** When you consider the aural experience, we can break it down into three separate categories to clarify the differences:

The Three Categories of Aural experience:

1. **HEARING** – is the most basic and natural part of the aural experience. It requires no effort. **Hearing simply means that we are aware of the sounds** that are being transported to our brain from our ears. Background noise that isn't created by and/or welcome by you, falls into this category. If you have ever sat in your living room and heard a bird or a lawnmower in the background, you were experiencing hearing. When you are working, and your coworker is typing and people are talking, your natural hearing is automatically at work.

2. **LISTENING** – is also a natural part of the aural experience, but where hearing happens automatically, listening requires some effort to clarify certain hearing points. When you focus your ears and brain on the sounds you wish to further evaluate and understand, you are listening. **With listening, we are giving closer attention to the sounds we choose to hear.** You might hear background noise, like traffic, but you give your attention to listen to music or certain lyrics.

3. **ACTIVE LISTENING** – is the third category and differs greatly because where the other two are natural functions, active listening is categorized as a skill. What separates active listening from the other two is conscious concentration. You must work at active listening by deliberately engaging your mind, eyes, ears, and other physical components.

   Active listening requires concentration, discipline, and 'being present' with your body, mind, eyes, and ears. Also, because active listing is indeed a skill, the Lion Leader spends quality time practicing this skill on a daily basis.

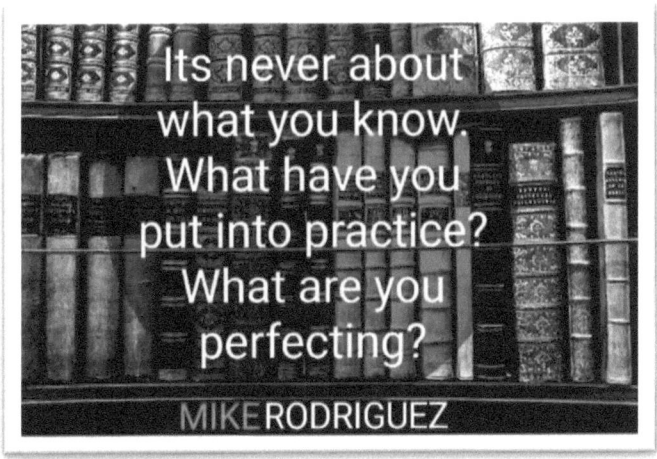

STRATEGIC CONVERSATIONS

When it comes to difficult conversations or what we call strategic conversations, here are the facts:
- **Almost 60 percent of employees in the U.S. have never received basic conflict resolution training.**
- **76 percent of employees who receive conflict management and dispute resolution training experience positive outcomes.** (2019 CPP Inc. Study)

Knowing this data, we can quickly conclude that the reason we fail at difficult conversations is because we aren't equipped, so we don't have a plan. Also, we can learn that when people are trained properly, they have a significantly greater chance for success. Reflecting on our previous knowledge of the culture and performance model, it is easy to see that when you have a 'culture heavy' team or a 'performance heavy' team that you will typically have greater instances of difficult conversations.

Most people get confused about the purpose and the implications of engaging in the art of communication. Your approach to situational communication should be taken very seriously, as it has a direct impact on employee productivity, motivation, engagement, and performance. Therefore, your communication strategy, or lack thereof, will have a tremendous impact on your overall business health. I have outlined six strategic steps, that when followed, can help you to have a successful strategic conversation.

Step 1. Identify the Matter at Hand
Is This a Conduct or Performance Matter?

If you need to have a difficult conversation with one of your direct reports, you need to first identify the basis of your meeting: This might sound easy or unnecessary, however, please know that there is a tremendous difference between a performance matter and a conduct matter. (It is critical that you understand and know how they are handled.)

Chapter II – The Power of Strategy

I have put together a short list to help you identify your particular matter at hand: (Note: This list is not comprehensive.)

CONDUCT	PERFORMANCE
Drugs & Alcohol Matters	Absence / Tardiness
Threats & Harassment	Low quality / Low Skill / Low Desire
Racial or Religion concerns	Missed Deadlines / targets
Theft or Lying	Poor / low performance
Physical or Mental Health matters	Attitude / Behavior / Disengaged
Conduct /policy Violations	Other policy violations

The Differences

Conduct Matters: violate a company policy/code of conduct or present a possible legal liability. They generally lead to corrective action, up to and including termination. This can happen for a first offense where there is no prior corrective action on record.

When problems occur in these areas, leaders are expected to engage your professional HR leadership team immediately. Conduct Matters should be considered:
- Critical Matters
- Addressed Immediately
- Will include your HR professional

Performance Matters: pertain to day-to-day operational issues, typically referring to substandard productivity in the areas of quality/results, quantity, speed, service, and even attendance/tardiness. When problems occur in these areas, leaders are expected to provide "workplace due process development" through Leadership skills, engagement, and communication.
- Standard Matter
- Addressed situationally
- Can be resolved with the leader

Don't be deceived between the two. Performance matters can, and sometimes do, evolve and/or escalate into conduct matters if not properly addressed and corrected. On a side note, if you are having a conversation commending someone, still stick with the facts. Don't overinflate what isn't great. You risk diluting performance standards.

Step 2. Schedule Time for a Conversation With the Person

This step might seem obvious to you or it might seem unnecessary. I can tell you with complete confidence that this step is strategic and is indeed, very necessary.

As a leader, you can and should understand that different meetings serve different purposes. If you aren't running your business this way, then you need to take note of the differences:

- **Team Meetings** serve as a time to plan together and get updates as a team.
- **Client Meetings** serve to understand, propose and align with those who seek to do business with you.
- **Corporate Events** serve to bring unity with your team community and to celebrate milestones.
- **1 on 1's** serve to address the needs and efforts of each individual team member.

Chapter II – The Power of Strategy

As you can see, you already separate your meetings based on the purpose of the meeting. When it comes to performance or conduct reviews, you must do the same. Hopefully, you wouldn't address a performance matter with a team member at a client meeting or a corporate event. And I suppose you would never address a conduct matter in a team meeting. With that, you should set aside a specific time to address a performance review or conduct matter with an individual outside any of the above-mentioned meetings. The reason we do this is to call to the attention that nonstandard behavior gets nonstandard attention! Corrective action needs personal attention.

When we don't separate performance and behavioral matters from standard workplace meetings, we blur the lines, degrading morale, culture, and performance. The core principle here is that if you don't dedicate time to address the matter now, in a private setting, I promise you that you will have to invest time later to address it, possibly in a public setting (think possible litigation).

What to do:
    a. DATE - Set a Date to meet with the person.
    b. TIME – Establish a start time (allocate 30 minutes).
    c. ENVIRONMENT – Choose your environment carefully: in person (preferably), or virtual (for remote team members), in the office/conference room. (Never choose a food shop for a conduct matter.)
    d. PLAN – Who will attend? What are the facts? What is the outcome of the meeting?

When conducting one of these meetings, ensure that you never give the impression of an interrogation or a hearing. The point is to create a neutral environment to emphasize the nature of the behavioral matter at hand, not to embarrass the person.

Step 3. Validate the Matter at Hand

You've set up your meeting and now you are ready. Your goal here is to review the 'what' behavior that is going on, so they can illuminate their own lightbulb. Effective communication starts with:

- **clarifying the behavioral matter, while**
- **separating the behavior from the person.**

This means that you will not take anything personally, nor will you make anything personal. You will also be aware of your mindset. If you are stressed, angry, or upset, set the meeting for another day. You must be aware of your tone and delivery to ensure you aren't coming across as accusatory or jaded. The goal here is for you to create an awareness of the behavioral matter in order to establish personal accountability. You will do this by asking questions, using objective, not subjective examples of their behavior. You must know **THE BIG TWO in every matter at hand:**

1. **What IS happening that SHOULDN'T BE, or**
2. **What ISN'T happening that SHOULD BE**

Then determine **the consequences** of any current or future behaviors that align with continuing instances of the matter.

Strategic Conversation Flow

1. Determine: **Performance (you) or ⟶ Conduct (HR)**
2. Meet: Clarify what they **"Are" or "Are NOT"** doing
3. Establish a **Plan for resolution (corrective or other)**
4. Introduce **Consequences** if no sustainable progress:
   1) Verbal warning 2) Written warning or 3) Final

(Not intended as legal advice. Please consult your attorney)

Chapter II – The Power of Strategy

I commit to embrace the POWER of Strategy!

What can I do to stay at the competitor mindset?

_____

_____

What are the Key 3 for Cognitive Preparation?

_____

_____

How can I become an Inside-Out thinker?

_____

_____

What can I alter or adjust to become a strategic, active listener?

_____

_____

Chapter II – The Power of Strategy

The overall losses
brought about by neglecting to strategize
can never be measured completely.

"The quality of candidates you bring in will be equivalent to the quality of time you put into evaluating your candidates."

Mike Rodriguez

Strategy to Evaluate Talent

Chapter III – Strategy to Evaluate Talent

The KIT Car

A counterfeit can be hard to spot. We often find that if we evaluate things on the outside to determine authenticity, we can almost always be deceived. This happens because great steps are usually taken to conceal what we know should not be seen. However, inevitably most counterfeits are usually exposed after a closer look.

A few years back, I was leaving a restaurant after having lunch with a friend. As we exited, I noticed a small group of people standing around a very expensive and unique, high-performance sports car that I believed to be a Lamborghini.

Being a man who appreciates this type of art, I soon found myself wandering over to take a closer look. As I approached the car, the small crowd started dispersing, so I walked around the car. This Lamborghini was magnificent and looked exactly like what I had seen on television. I was impressed. As I approached the driver's side, the owner called out, "Do you like it?" "I do" I responded. "It's a fine automobile, what line of work are you in?" He responded by telling me that he was in the dry-cleaning business. I probed a bit further, clarifying "So you own a chain of stores?" "No, he replied." I was confused. That answer did not seem to align with owning such a high-end car.

Chapter III – Strategy to Evaluate Talent

At that moment he started the car, and it put out an unfamiliar sound; instead of the unmistakable purring-rumble associated with this type of car, it sounded more like your standard automobile. At that point, he looked over at me and noticed the puzzled look on my face. It was then that he looked side to side before he responded with a sneaky smile, "It's a kit car." "A kit car?" I responded, "Yes," he said, the shell is a replica of a Lambo, but the inside is a Volkswagen.

Apparently, this man truly desired to have this type of car for show. He had gone to great lengths to change the exterior of the car, to imitate the original, but he had neglected to change the inside. Although it met the external, visual standards, this was not in fact a real Lamborghini. It was a fake. Anyone with an ear ready to pay attention would have noticed that the sound coming out of this car was not in line with what that type of car should have been producing. Apparently, this man wasn't willing to take the steps necessary to make the insides match the exterior, but he did at least confess his deception. The truth is that this car was all show and no go.

When it comes to evaluating candidates, you are also going to find "all show and no go" people. They look sharp and talk the game. They look like performance people, but inside they don't have what it truly takes.

When it comes to evaluating talent, remember that it's what's inside that matters.

TALENT EVALUATION

People abuse, misuse, and interchange the words, hiring, onboarding, interviewing, vetting, and screening. These words can and usually do mean very different things to different people and organizations. To the untrained leader, they accept them as cliché or worse, they put them all in the same category. When this happens, you will have an ineffective process to evaluate your talent. For example, you may have been asked to interview someone. Interviewing by definition is a Q&A format to get information; someone asks questions and the other person answers those questions. But what information are you getting and how does it apply to the overall success of the organization or the ability of the candidate to qualify to fit the role?

This is a standardized flawed approach in our world today that usually ends with "I liked them" or "I don't think they will fit in." Both of these answers are incorrect because they are based on emotion and opinion; they aren't strategic.

Talent Evaluation, on the other hand, is strategically designed to evaluate the relevant expertise and skills of the candidate. Our purpose is to find a performance and cultural match for your open role; not to find people that 'you like' or who you 'think are good.'

Yes, we have defined your candidates as "talent," because you are in fact evaluating their talent (skills or gifts) to help you with your objectives. You are evaluating talent:

- Through your established process (Quality control)
- Against your established requirements (Critical fit)
- Against what they say (Prove it)
- Against other talent presented to you (Best candidate)
- As a team (Consensus)

Chapter III – Strategy to Evaluate Talent

The Initial Vetting Process
Talent evaluation is a process, not an event.

Many people today dread "interviewing" so they rush through it, simply looking for people 'they like' or who will 'fit in,' using personal experience or opinion as their key premise for hiring. When we don't have a process to depend on, we tend to make these types of rookie mistakes and depend on ourselves. In some cases, we might be rushed by an eager leader who falsely believes that hiring any candidate now is better than having an empty role. (Rushing is ignorance at its finest.) Remember, there are four core risks with talent evaluation:

- Making decisions based on emotions (Leads to failure)
- Not dedicating the appropriate time to evaluate (Rushed)
- Not following a proven process (Relies on emotion)
- Not having the right skills to evaluate (Leads to failure)

The talent evaluation system is a multi-stage progression that starts with:

1. **Strategic Planning** – The power of strategy behind planning your talent evaluation strategy is that you can:
   - Establish standards
   - Self-vet and stop bad candidates
   - Create a system for red flags
   - Prevent poor talent from infiltrating your ranks

The purpose of planning helps you to remember that you are establishing criteria as a team to find those with the competitor mindset. When you remember that 70% of people are complacent, 20% are complainers, and only 10% are competitors, you can understand that you have your work cut out for you.

You must also remember that you have a responsibility to sustain, build, and balance your culture, performance, and results. Your hiring goal always starts with the facts that:

- You have a need,
- You require qualified talent to help you attain that need.

Chapter III – Strategy to Evaluate Talent

2. **Sourcing** – The public call-out to see who is a fit. Now that you have established your needs and the criteria you require from candidates to fit that need, you can start sourcing. **Referrals** are not always your best bet. Yes, it's good that someone on your team knows the referred talent, but statistically, most people only refer their friends, neighbors, and family as a gesture of good will. Usually because the persons need a job, not because they are the best candidate. Your employee typically isn't aware of their skills, work ethic, and ability to succeed in the role.
Public Call out – Is usually your best bet. This type of sourcing (social media, job boards, networking) is as effective as a referral, but you can actually see who takes initiative to respond or reach out to you.

3. **Resume Vet** – is scanning the document sent to look for the minimum requirement you established. Once you put your 'public call out,' people should start reaching out. Usually, you will get many resumes, but you should pay close attention to those who aren't afraid to call you directly, especially in public-facing roles. Vetting a resume should be assigned to a qualified individual on your team who was part of the planning process. They should know what the established core vet minimums are. The minimums can and should include criteria such as:
   - Tenure
   - Skills
   - Experience and Expertise
   - Industry, or
   - Other variables that you established as core vet minimums during the resume vet process.

After the resume scan, your team member assigned to vet, needs to capture responses into two categories:
   - Those who meet the established minimum requirements
   - Those who don't

Remember YOU are not your target audience! Meaning, just because you like, think, or feel, good about a person, doesn't make them a qualified candidate. None of us are clairvoyant or have E.S.P., so assuming you know something others don't, is not solid intuition, it is naïve arrogance. Raise the bar, never lower it.

Use your 'gut feeling' for eating, not for talent evaluation.

4. **Vetting Call** – Is a live confirmation to confirm the minimum requirements; not to work through emotional excuses. This is accomplished with a candidate from your team. The vetting team member should conduct a brief phone call:
    - Ask key minimum requirement questions
    - Validate that the candidate meets or exceeds the requirements, and
    - Clarify if we will progress the candidate through to the Q.E.S.T. Interview stages.

The CORE 4 STRATEGIC COMPONENTS

Once you have initially vetted your candidates, it's time to run the 4 Core diagnostic components. Unless you are wealthy or retired, everybody needs to (and should) work. Job hunting is difficult for people because most are playing defense to defend their position. This means that people are more likely to put on their best face and tell you what you want to hear, because let's face it, they need a job or want another job.

Throughout our research, we have determined that there are 4 core strategic components that allow you to gain a better basis for evaluating the candidate. These diagnostic components are designed to strategically clarify often neglected details that have a great influence on the ability of the candidate to stay, succeed, and thrive.

Chapter III – Strategy to Evaluate Talent

1. **Catalyst to Change – Why are they looking?**
   If you are out of work and you need a job, you might not want me to know; but I need to know why you are looking. My team performance depends on it! There are 4 key reasons why people are looking for work:
   - **Situational** – Something happened
   - **Personal** – Looking for career growth, not a fit
   - **Conflict** – Personalities, not respected
   - **Corporate** – Need better benefits, salary, career path

   Your goal is to effectively address these two points:
   Clarification Point: You aren't looking for fault. Can what happened where they were, happen 'here' (your team) as well?

   Philosophical Point: People shouldn't run FROM things; they should run TO things.

2. **Catalyst to Resolve: What are they looking for/to do?**
   If you can reasonably determine why they are looking, now it's time to figure out what they are looking for. Most people can sell you on why they are looking, but many more lack transparency in revealing what they are truly looking to do. Factoring in the points above, does their answer provide resolution to why they are looking?
   - **Situational** – Are we just a resource or an outcome?
   - **Personal** – What can they do here that will 'better' both of us?
   - **Conflict** – What will be different here with us?
   - **Corporate** – What problem do we solve together?

   Your goal is to effectively address these two points:
   Clarification Point: We aren't looking for clichés; will working with us really solve something for both of us?

   Philosophical Point: Are they ready to change personally, or are they just ready to change jobs?

Chapter III – Strategy to Evaluate Talent

3. **Vetting Process: Why YOU/Why US? (Q.E.S.T.)**
   The vetting process is where we use QEST (coming up next), to effectively evaluate the candidates:
   - **Qualification** – What skills do you bring/do we need?
   - **Experience/Expertise** – Will we both gain value/uplift?
   - **Strategic Thinker** – Does mindset and personality match and benefit our culture?
   - **Testing** – Can they do what they say they can do AND can they do it well.

Your goal is to effectively address these two points:
Clarification Point: We should not be too rigid to our standards, but we also should not compromise.

Philosophical Point: If they aren't a fit now, expect more issues later.

4. **Vetting Outcome: Are we a fit? (Q.E.S.T.)**
   The vetting outcome continues with QEST to effectively validate the candidates:
   - **Qualification** – They are in fact qualified for the role.
   - **Experience/Expertise** – They can assimilate well without resistance.
   - **Strategic Thinker** – They are a fit and can bring value.
   - **Testing** – We validate the skills they have claimed.

Your goal is to effectively address these two points:
Clarification Point: We aren't looking for perfection, but we also must not compromise.

Philosophical Point: When in doubt, maybe means no.

When you ask a question, really listen to the answer, and seek clarification instead of preparing to ask your next question.

Chapter III – Strategy to Evaluate Talent

Q.E.S.T. INTERVIEW STAGES

The purpose of the Q.E.S.T. Stages of Talent Evaluation is that they serve as a solid structure and flow to evaluate your talent. You are on a "QUEST" to not only evaluate, but also to bring the best talent into your team and culture. The goal is also to equip the evaluator with the core strategy of:

Ask - questions as your basic strategic approach, relevant to QEST

Listen - Actively listen to their answers and avoid cliched answers or generalizations.

Observe - how they answer, posture, voice inflection, personality, tone, and tempo.

Clarify – Anything that doesn't make sense or isn't clear.

Objectives:
- Do we align? (your organization and the talent)
- Can you do, what you do…HERE.

NOTE: Each stage needs to be handled by 4 different leaders if at all possible: Leaders A, B, C, D/You. I cover these steps in greater detail in my live training sessions.

Stage 1. Interview - with Leader A
Q- Qualifications - Can they do the job?

I was unqualified for my first leadership job. I lacked the skills and experience required, so I failed. One time I hired a young lady that looked, spoke, and acted like a pro. The problem was that she did not have any experience or any transferrable skills to excel. In fact, she wanted to be in HR, and she told me. She wasn't qualified for the job and she failed.

Your goal at this stage is to avoid the mistakes I made. In this stage, you are only to focus on finding out if they can do the job: Are they qualified? Not just that they want to do the job, but have they been doing this type of work successfully? Are they able to give details, outline processes, and share relevant facts that validate they are indeed qualified? If they are in fact qualified to do the job, then you progress them to Stage 2. If not, you pass on the candidate.

Chapter III – Strategy to Evaluate Talent

Stage 2. Interview - with Leader B
E - Expertise vs Experience – Relevant success

I once had a pipe leaking under my sink that I couldn't figure out how to fix, so I called in an expert, a plumber. After looking under my sink for twenty minutes, the plumber pulled his head out and said, "Sir, you are mistaken, I've looked everywhere and I can assure you, that you don't have a leak." I quickly responded, "Then how do you explain all of the water damage under the sink?" He calmly stated back, "I don't know, but sir, I have been a plumber for twenty-five years, you are going to have to trust me, you don't have a leak." I thought for a moment and then realized I had turned off the water to the sink. I quickly turned the water back on causing the pipe to start dripping again. The man yelled out "Ok there it is! I can fix it now." This man had told me with conviction that he had been a plumber for over two decades! The problem here wasn't that he had twenty years of experience as a plumber. The problem here was that he had not worked to develop his expertise during his years, therefore, he was by no means an expert. He was just a man with many years of experience being a plumber.

In stage 2, you are evaluating the accomplishments of the candidate 'during their tenure.' What have they accomplished? Your goal here is to only focus on evaluating their relevant expertise, finding out their level of skill development and successes. Like our plumber friend, they might have been doing the job for twenty years, which is considered experience, but the real question is have they been consistently successful? Are they able to give details, outline successes relevant to the job, and share facts that validate they are indeed at or pursuing a level of expertise? If they, in fact, do possess the expertise, you progress them to stage 3, if not, you pass.

Stage 3. Interview – with Leader C
S - Strategic Thinking – Mindset, Communication

My friend once hired an experienced salesman who couldn't or wouldn't look for alternate ways to close opportunities. He was stubborn, closed-minded, and limited in his thoughts and routines. He was not a strategic thinker; he was an excuse maker who constantly sought out others to validate his cause.

In this stage, you are evaluating if the candidate is or can be a strategic thinker and to avoid those who aren't. Are they willing to get uncomfortable to improve and find new ways to succeed? Your goal here is to only focus on evaluating their strategic thinking. Here you are finding out their level of thought and insight in dealing with relevant job role situations, problems, emotions, and people. Everyone says they are a strategic thinker, but can they prove it? Are they able to provide insightful, relevant, and genuine answers to open-ended questions? Can they describe how and why they do what they do and how they did what they claim they have done? If they in fact can show you through interactive dialogue that they are a strategic thinker, then you progress them to stage 4. If not, pass.

Stage 4. Interview- with Leader D
T – Testing – Live work sample/Preso/Business plan

It is chronic in our world to hire people on 'gut feeling' or based on experience. Testing is the most neglected of the stages and is by far the most important. If the candidate says they can do the job, and do it well, then they have a responsibility to show you. With that, you have a responsibility to test them.

Testing is when you have the candidate actually do what it is that you are hiring them to do. In this stage, you are evaluating the candidate in real-time situations, putting their skills to work in a live environment. Your goal here is to only focus on evaluating their skills live, to find out their specific skills required for the job. You can also determine how they deal with situations, emotions, and people.

Most say they can do a job, but with stage 4 testing, they are put to the test. Are they able to walk through a work sample they created? Can they conduct a demo, a role play, or a presentation? If they can't do it here, and they are all show and no go, now is the best time to find out. If they in fact have shown that they can pass the testing properly, then the next step is to meet as a team to evaluate and compare your findings.

If you have red flags, determine if you need clarification or if you will pass on the candidate. If the red flags need further clarification, call the candidate up and ask them to clarify. Review their answer with the team to gain agreement and approval. During your evaluation, how did the candidate measure up:

- **Did they pass the QEST Stages?**
- **Did they meet or exceed the requirements?**
- **Are they qualified?**
- **Have they been successful?**
- **Can they validate they can do the job?**
- **Did they successfully pass the live tests?**
- **Are they the right fit for your team?**

If you all aren't in agreement, find out why, based on facts, and make a firm decision. If you decide that all of you are in agreement, then make an offer.

VALUE vs PERSONAL WORTH

Making a compensation offer can get complicated when you let emotions rule. Offers are simple: they are a financial proposal, based on
- The performance value and level of expertise the candidate brings to your organization,
This amount must be factored in against...
- The budgeted expectations for the role.

Yes, contrary to public opinion, you should pay someone with a higher career value and greater expertise more than someone who has less expertise and lower career value. I am an established professional speaker. Expect to pay for the value and expertise I bring to your organization. If you have a low budget, don't ask me to lower my value. I would encourage you to consider a lower value speaker to meet your budget. As my mentor, the late great Jim Rohn said, "It's not that something is expensive, it's that you just can't afford it." So, don't wish it were cheaper, wish you were better! This same principle applies to your candidates when evaluating talent. Learn to separate personal worth from value.

Performance Value: What they have proven, established, accomplished, or built. The measurable expertise, transferrable skills, and established value that a candidate WILL bring to the organization.

Personal Worth: What they think about themselves. What the candidate HOPES to receive based on how they view their level of experience or what they subjectively feel they deserve based on personal opinion.

When it comes to compensation, some might consider their personal worth to be in the high six figures. Sure, why not. Think highly of yourself. However, their performance value might (and probably will) be considerably less. Be fair, but not in the way the world demands.

Fair compensation means relevant pay for relevant expertise, not fair pay for all. The fair pay for all model detracts from your experts, and ironically brings an unfair parity to your organization. In other words, a recent college graduate should not be paid the same compensation as a candidate with five years of proven expertise. If these two people are being considered for the same role, either bring the expert in at a higher role or bring the college graduate in at a lower role. Simply stated, the expert will bring greater value than the novice, and therefore should be compensated accordingly.

Final Tips
- When in doubt, maybe means no.
- Effective teams and results are attributed to better people, not more people
- You must put in the time necessary to evaluate the candidates you bring in. If you don't, I promise you that you will put in more time managing a performance plan to move them out later.
- Always hire based on Q.E.S.T., never hire based on personal attributes. Skills perform, not attributes.
- Don't seek equal pay, seek compensation based on performance value.

EMERGING vs FOUNDATIONAL LEADERS

At some point, you will have a major change in your team. Either you will need to hire solid outside talent to help you scale to the next level (a better option is to actively develop your current team), or you will need to hire from within. There is no time like the present to prepare your existing talent. You must equip those who show the desire, aptitude, and commitment with the expertise to become a Lion Leader. As mentioned previously, you should already be evaluating your current talent, and be aware of who is actively taking the initiative to pursue The BIG 3!

The BIG 3!
As mentioned, these are the core components to success for any person you should evaluate.
Skills – Who is going up and beyond to learn, grow and work towards expertise? We must keep developing and gaining skills.
Resources – Who uses your tools and uses them properly? Do they also teach, coach, and help others along the way?
Desire – Who has blatantly told you that they are committed to the team and to the greater cause?

Within your pride, the ones who step up and meet the QEST criteria should be considered first. You shouldn't have to go to your future leaders. They will let you know that they are all in. You will always have two categories of internal candidates:

Emerging Leaders

These are the leaders within your team who have shown and have verbally stated that they desire to lead and create a positive influence. They might not have the skill, but if they have the ability and desire to lead, then put them into a formal leadership mentoring program or assign them a gateway leadership position (Team lead, etc.). Your Emerging Leaders fit into two categories:
- **Those who stay for a committed time**, to help lead and influence, but the person has other long-term career plans in another calling.

Chapter III – Strategy to Evaluate Talent

- **Those who commit to emerge** within your organization long term, within progressive leadership roles, to build a path to become a…

Foundational Leaders

The Foundational Leader is the person who is ALL IN! They are committed to your organization, people, and greater cause for the long term. They will be a part of your foundational growth! This person must not only have the desire, but they must have the qualifications and expertise as outlined within Q.E.S.T. If you have to go to the person and ask if they want to pursue a foundational career, they probably aren't a foundational leader.

THE PRINCIPLE OF MOVING PEOPLE UP OR OUT

Just as you are always evaluating talent and future leaders, you must also adopt the mindset of moving people up or moving them out. This does not mean you run people off. I have always said that **any inexperienced leader can fire anyone, but it takes a true Lion Leader to help someone realize their potential and grow.**

Moving Up! The concept of moving up means that you are committed to moving people "Up." Up within your business, or Up from a performance plan and into new success. This requires time, interest, patience, and focus on the BIG 3!

Moving Out means that you have provided all of the resources to help them succeed, and all of the skill development training adequate for success, BUT…they aren't showing the desire to succeed, therefore, they have in fact made the decision to move out of your organization. Your job now is to help them move out based on the decision they have made to not be a part of your team. A lion leader provides all of the support as outlined above, but we understand that when someone chooses not to use the BIG 3, then they are choosing not to be a part of our culture and mission. We then have a responsibility to them and to our current team to simply help them move out. This is not a semantic, it is an honest pride principle.

You are building your culture through everything that you do. What culture are you building?

Chapter III – Strategy to Evaluate Talent

I commit to becoming a better leader!

What are the 4 Core Strategic components?

_____

_____

I will follow the Q.E.S.T. criteria to evaluate talent.

Q_____

E_____

S_____

T_____

What is the difference between experience & expertise?

_____

_____

What can I alter or adjust to become a better leader of my people?

_____

_____

Chapter IV – Strategically Adapting to Change

> "Course Corrections
> are the required component
> for change."
>
> Mike Rodriguez

Strategically Adapting to Change

Chapter IV – Strategically Adapting to Change

If you really want to change the behavior of your team, start by changing your own behavior first. Change is a constant part of our world. If you aren't anticipating change or at least prepared to adjust when it happens, you will become an emotional wreck and your people will disengage. When we are faced with challenges due to changes, the next rule to remember is that although something has changed, your established core principles should never change. Change is the opportunity to evaluate your current methodologies which will probably change as you make course corrections. Remember, our methods might change, but your principles never should.

THE M.A.I.L. PRINCIPLE

When a snowstorm hits a town prone to winter weather, even though several feet of snow might cover the road, the mail is still delivered. The postal system principle is that they are still committed to getting the mail from point A (the originator) to point B (your mailbox). The carrier might transport the mail in a larger vehicle, or it might be delayed while taking another course. In other words, their methods might change due to the adverse circumstances, but they adhere to their principle of committed delivery of the mail.

In leadership, your principles might be holding planning calls and strategic sessions, running board meetings, and hosting 1-1s. However, during a crisis, if you can't use your conventional or traditional "methods," then you must adapt to new methods in order to adjust. This is called your M.A.I.L. Principle. The M.A.I.L. Principle is your commitment to deliver on your key principles as an organization, no matter what.

M - Model
A - Assist
I - Inspect
L - Lead

Chapter IV – Strategically Adapting to Change

In the case of a snowstorm that impacts your organization, you will still run meetings (Principle), but you might run them over the phone or a virtual platform (Methods). Your M.A.I.L. Principle will be non-negotiable. Whatever is going on, you commit to finding a way to make things happen. Your organization should create your own M.A.I.L. principle, meaning during the worst of circumstances, you know your principles and you can identify new methods in order to fulfill your commitment to meet those principles. Following the M.A.I.L. principle, means that you know your targets and therefore you can use the power of strategy in order to plan and commit to align.

M- Model: Be the Example

A core rule in leadership is that **people will always follow what you do before they do what you say.** As the leader, YOU set the tempo to determine if people decide to be engaged or disengaged & to what degree. If you are frightened, it will show, and your people will scatter. If you are disconnected, your people will disconnect, and if you are less than honest, your people will leave. However, if you set the example and establish a model of being honest and optimistic, with a strategic plan, people will respond positively. Here are a few things you can do:

- Set new routines and create a culture of confidence.
- Improve internal workflow communication.
- Communicate both the good and the bad. People fear silence and will always assume the worst.
- Be optimistic, but also be truthful. If things are going to be challenging for a while, let people know.
- Help everyone see the bigger picture (Philosophy). Remind them why they are here and remind them that you are committed to your principles.
- Talk facts, not opinions.

Chapter IV – Strategically Adapting to Change

A- Assist: Be a Support Resource

Change, under most circumstances, creates fear, uncertainty, and doubt which can be paralyzing. Your people need to know that they aren't going through change alone. As a leader, you must be proactive to anticipate challenges before they happen. Consider the risks and factor in how certain people will react.

Using the power of strategy, you can build on your philosophy of success principles to figure out, as a team, how you can work through difficulties together. Be responsive to the questions and requests of your team, knowing that any interpretation of a disconnect will immediately start to kill your culture. Make time for live interaction with teams and groups to keep them updated with news, progress, plans, actions, and results. When you communicate, talk about forward-thinking concepts. In other words, don't live in the past, and don't engage in conversations about negative "what ifs" (What if we fail?). Instead, shift to forward-thinking concepts to help the team to consider positive "what ifs" (What if we succeed?).

Finally, don't be fake, by being falsely optimistic, but be convicted by your past successes, your current strategic plans, and your ability to prevail. Encourage your team, ask questions, and seek input, and reassure them that you are all committed to the greater mission. Let them know that you need them! Typically, the more you genuinely inspire those under your care, the greater the team performance.

I-Inspect: Ensure Principles Stay Intact

According to a 2015 Gallup survey, nearly 70% of employees are not actively engaged in their work. If this high percentage is happening during normal times, you must consider what the risks of engagement are during change or difficult times? Understanding that your principles are the fundamental truths that serve as your foundation, simply planning and trusting is a weak strategy. You must inspect what you expect. People are creatures of habit and after any initial flash of ideas, rollout, or planning, most will figure that if they aren't being held accountable, that it is ok to slow. Seventy percent of people are complacent, not doing any more than is required of them unless they are asked, but they are always being pulled to do less if they can get away with it. Most people don't do this intentionally, but it is natural human behavior to slow. The risk with this is that your principles along with your methods will be compromised. Our Methods (How we do things) might change, but we never compromise our principles (What we do & Why we are doing it). Here are a few strategies to consider, by asking yourself and your leaders:

- Are we treating others with respect?
- Are we showing up? (meetings, 1-1s, emails)
- Are we meeting the needs of our people and our clients?
- Are we doing our jobs? (action, timeframes, deadlines, targets)

L - Lead Your People!

Obstacles are an opportunity to test commitment, skills and desire, and your ability to lead! During any difficulty, ask yourself, Am I all in? And be honest. If not, then you must adjust and do what it takes, or adjust by removing yourself as you are a liability. Your people need a leader and facing difficult change is not the time to learn how to lead. Don't be a source of resistance or division. Many leaders react poorly under stress and revert to emotions of fear, anger, impatience, or empathy and agreement.

Now is the time to be bold and lead like a lion, to be immovable in your principles and be a source of strength to your people. Here are a few things you can do:

- Hold weekly team meetings for progress updates.
- Hold weekly 1:1s with key leaders to share updates and catch issues.

Chapter IV – Strategically Adapting to Change

- Have weekly company comradery calls (just through the change), then move to monthly calls. These should be team bonding, inspirational updates, and trainings.
- Be a source of positive refreshment! (True Competitor!)
- Remind yourself of where your organization will be after the change.

**"During difficult times,
you don't take the actions you want to,
you take the actions you need to."**

**Remember the M.A.I.L. Principle:
Always deliver!**

Chapter IV – Strategically Adapting to Change

USING THE BIG PICTURE TO LEAD

Success is a team effort—one that each team member should participate in willingly. Profound change is most successful when regular people work together to create extraordinary results, guided by leaders who have established a clear vision. This is called vision – towards the BIG PICTURE!

The Sandstorm

If you've ever been in or seen a sandstorm it is a frightening experience. It's not so much that the storm is present, as much as it is the effects that the person in the sandstorm experiences. In a sandstorm, the individual is fully engulfed in the blowing sand, slowly becoming paralyzed to their own thoughts. As they attempt to keep their senses, they find that they become more disoriented. It is an emotional game of illusion.

The individual starts to become more afraid as they realize that they cannot see, hear, or find direction. As the sand blows in their face, they now find that they have difficulty breathing and they start to lose control. Is this a certain death experience? It can be if you don't think strategically.

Chapter IV – Strategically Adapting to Change

When a person or an organization goes through any sort of change, people can experience similar symptoms. They might not be able to see, hear, or know the direction. It can cause fear to take over and lead people to believe that the end is near.

But remember that change, like a sandstorm, is only temporary. The event will eventually end. In addition, you can only survive a sandstorm and change, if you think strategically and take control. Here is what you can do:

- Know and accept that the situation is temporary.
- Don't freak out, stay on track to survive long term.
- Don't focus on what you can't do, focus on what you can do and get it done.
- Do your part and don't let the sandstorm overtake your mind, eyes, or let it inside.
- Change your focus to view the sandstorm as a temporary distraction, not as a terminal event.

> **When you view change through the small lens of fear, you adjust change to fit the fear.**

Crisis Creates Fudd
- F – Fear: False emotions appearing real.
- U – Uncertainty: Focus on possibilities, not certainties.
- D – Doubt: Comprising your principles.
- D – Disconnect: Abandoning strategies for emotions.

Instead of allowing FUDD to cloud your mind, think strategically and accept change as a **Merge Crisis.** A Merge Crisis is a steady life or business foundation that has collided with another new life or business foundation. Having to work at home during a pandemic is a merge crisis: Your personal life foundation has now merged with your business life foundation.

Chapter IV – Strategically Adapting to Change

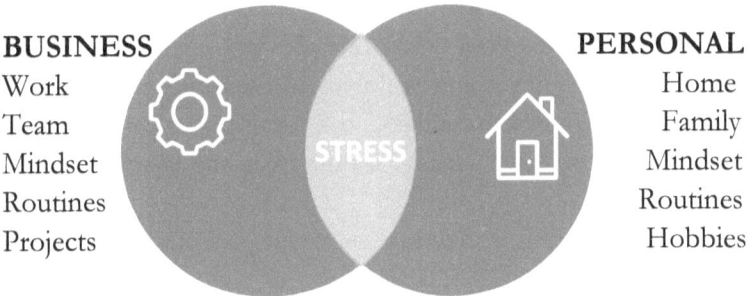

BUSINESS
Work
Team
Mindset
Routines
Projects

PERSONAL
Home
Family
Mindset
Routines
Hobbies

Merge Crisis:
Life Foundations blended by an abrupt change.

THE PARADIGM SHIFT

The first step to dealing with any foundational change is to fundamentally create a change in the way things are viewed (philosophy). This is also called a paradigm shift. You do this so you can fully exercise the power of a new strategy. You start to view your principles as permanent and non-negotiable, while evaluating your current methodologies (how you do things).

When you make a paradigm shift, you are challenging your own thoughts to get out of your complacent mindset and to move to your full competitor mindset.

You must evaluate:
- How we do things vs how we must start doing them.
- What are the new actions we must take?
- What are the new risks?
- What new resources will we need?
- What new skills will we need?
- What resistance people will give and how to mitigate it?
- What we will do to make course corrections along the way?

Chapter IV – Strategically Adapting to Change

Create A Framework for Success!
1. Validate that your core principles will stay intact.
2. Establish new methodologies and train people.
3. Establish new boundaries for communication.
4. Set clear expectations for outcomes and ensure they are met.
5. Have healthy conversations about your strategic plans.

Remember that when you are facing change, that what you say now, and do now, is what you will face when the dust settles.

Strategize a New Picture

Yes, you have core principles and yes you are headed to your key targets, but people must be able to see where they are short term and where they are going long term. Prior to your change, you had established the company vision, and all were on board. Now with the winds of change, people must be able to clearly see the new direction.

Once when I was flying to NYC, we started experiencing tremendous turbulence. Everyone could feel the plane moving up and down and side to side as the pilot tried to find a better route. For those of us who were experienced travelers, we knew what the pilot was doing. For everyone else, they sat in fear wondering if the plane was going to crash. Finally, after about 5 minutes, the pilot made an announcement. He calmly stated that we were experiencing heavy turbulence and that he was searching for a calmer path to fly. He assured everyone that all was ok. He also added that although we might make a slight change to our flight path, we would still arrive at our destination safely, but maybe a few minutes late.

What the pilot had accomplished by commutating with us is that he painted a new positive picture. He allowed people to calm their nerves. Everyone relaxed as they were able to see and believe the new picture.

Chapter IV – Strategically Adapting to Change

When you encounter difficulties as a team, you don't change your targets, you simply change how you get there. BUT you must communicate and paint a new picture for those traveling with you so they can feel confident in where they are going. This is another example of the power of strategy: **You must communicate what is going on in your mind and then share how you plan to execute it.**

When people are aware of the new strategy, then they can buy into the new strategy, but it takes time. We call this transition a Merge Crisis Curve. It outlines how people adjust. The stages are as follows:

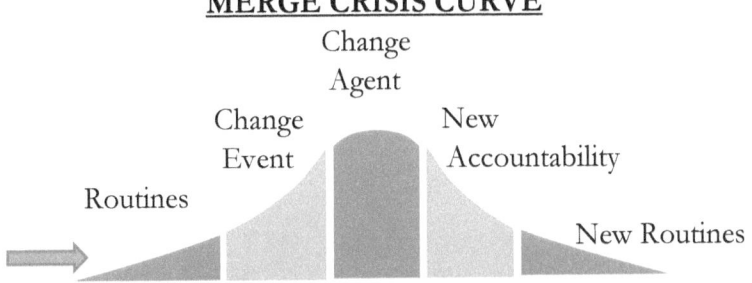

Comfortable > Emotional > Resistant > Adjustment > Acceptance

When working through change or a merge crisis, remember that there is a tremendous difference between managing and leading. Managers create routines and policy, while leaders focus on establishing strategic, vision-based results. With that, it is important for the leader to constantly evaluate and strategize based on the team's needs and direction, even if they must do it quickly. An initial weak team strategy executed over the short term might be better than a strong strategy that is wrong for the team.

Don't over strategize and don't mistake meeting and planning as an achievement. It is easy to get faked out by being busy, but the real question is, "What are you busy doing?"

Chapter IV – Strategically Adapting to Change

Are you being productive? The critical components of working through change are:
1. All actions must be thought through and vetted.
2. Strategize with others outside of your team if you are still unsure.
3. Use and exhaust what you already have first, before you add a new component.

When adapting to change, you must always consider different viewpoints. Your way isn't always the best way or the only way. However, always go with expertise over input from someone with a title or position who lacks previous long-term success. You must also collaborate, as this is the premise of a strong team strategy. You will always make higher and better-quality decisions together. Finally, participate in strategic planning. Don't just listen in and be a spectator. Your insight is needed!

RECALIBRATE

Change requires adjustment. You have to ask yourself "Do we want to be defined by the marketplace or do we want to define the marketplace? You must recalibrate.

First, you must recalibrate your agenda, to change the team's thinking. When faced with change, it is easy to seek out information that supports individual beliefs, while ignoring information that contradicts those beliefs. This is called confirmation bias. As we discussed previously, it is a chronic culture killer especially during change, when emotions are high. Winston Churchill said:

"A pessimist sees difficulty in every opportunity. The optimist sees opportunity in every difficulty."

Therefore, your core principle to adapt must always be to choose facts over opinions.

Recalibration Points (Course Corrections)

Growth Points – New things that we can start doing that we haven't been doing that will allow us to realize new growth.

Shaping Points – Current things that we are doing, but we need to adjust and improve in order to better align with our new objectives. We might need to do more of these if they are healthy for us, less if they are good, but we are wasting efficiency, or change how we do them altogether if there is a better way.

Anchor points – Things that we do that are holding us back and create resistance. You will need to put strategic thought into this area and have deep conversations with your team. These are the items that people will fight to hold on to, emotionally claiming: "We've always done it this way!" In reality, those people simply don't want to change and as a result, they are holding you back. Truth alert! Some people on your team might be the anchor points you need to address.

Recalibration Process

Once you determine your possible recalibration points, you must start the strategic recalibration process as follows:

1. Observe: How are we doing and what things fall into the recalibration point categories?
2. Ask: What can we start, stop, or change about our current methodologies, processes, or systems?
3. Evaluate: What are the risks and benefits of making the changes we propose?
4. Strategize: Plan together what and how and when you will implement the new methodologies.

Chapter IV – Strategically Adapting to Change

5. Apply: Take action to put the infrastructure in place to support the new strategic changes.

Recalibrate Your Meetings to Become Strategic Sessions

You must move from being a business-centered, people supported culture, to a people-centered, business supported model. Start with implementing strategic Sessions:
- **Prepare for Sessions Properly** – Don't just throw things together and follow the same routines.
- **Allow Adequate Time** – If you don't need an hour don't ask for an hour. If you need two hours, don't jam the content into an hour.
- **Relevant Purpose** – An efficient session should properly and adequately address the topic at hand, answer questions, gain agreement, assign tasks, and close. Never mix content or topics.
- **Actions Items** – Never leave a meeting without knowing who is assigned what, and when the item is expected. When you fail to plan, you plan to fail.

As a leader, your core goal is to help your people move from a ME Mindset to a WE Mindset.
ME – I'm here to make money, do my job, and survive.
WE – I'm here to grow our business, build our culture, improve our performance, and increase our results!
You must also change the chatter of the culture, knowing that we become what we put into our minds.

Culture change starts at the individual level.

Chapter IV – Strategically Adapting to Change

SIX FOUNDATIONAL LEADERSHIP TRUTHS

1. **You cannot force values onto a person** – by implementing a policy that people must be honest, kind, or non-biased. This sounds good on the surface, but it will fail. You are not the humanity values police and you cannot control personal values. They are the core of who someone is, and the person must desire to change.

2. **Focus on the outcome, more than the policy** – You are going to need to recalibrate along your journey to success. You will need to make adjustments. Don't be so grounded in your policy that you miss an opportunity to work outside of the policy and grow. Don't just be flexible, adjusting for the moment and then going back to how things were. You must be pliable, adjusting, changing, and retaining your new form. Bendy straws are flexible, clay is pliable.

3. **More is lost from indecision, than from the wrong decision** – Yes, you can over-strategize. Waiting to start or procrastinating is always more of a liability than taking a new temporary action. When you act, you can learn from your decision and quickly make course corrections. Typically, when we wait, it costs us more as we delay progress, sometimes for years, working with failing systems.

4. **Reports and data mean nothing without review** – Yes, you are called to be a strategic leader and focus on facts, logic, and data, but you must also put your new knowledge into place. Here is the catch: how does the data apply to your people? If you are going to ask for reports and capture data, then review it and use it as a team to create a new outcome.

Chapter IV – Strategically Adapting to Change

5. **Focus on solutions, not emotions –**
    People are going to come to you with issues, sometimes in tears, wanting to get resolutions for their emotions. Emotions are important, but don't let them influence you. Instead, work to address a reasonable solution that will resolve or reconcile the issue that is making someone emotional.

6. **Make logical choices for tomorrow, not just today –**
    Remember, there is one constant: change. What worked for you in the past or what is working today, probably won't work for you tomorrow. In fact, it might not even be relevant. Make sure that your strategic thought and planning factor in where you will be and what will be needed to support you in the future.

The principles in this book rely on the middle point of strategy to 'bridge' philosophy with tactics. This allows you to become a strategic Lion Leader. Now when you face any issue at your organization, people, culture, or performance, you have a plan. You will go back and visit your philosophy to determine how and why you and/or your team view your situation the way you do. After a deep conversation, you can now work together to strategically plan on new ways to purposefully re-work what you will start doing differently. This middle bride of strategic planning prepares you for your final step. You can now take your new and improved actions on your new strategic plans to generate new, better, and greater results. You can do things with clarity and purpose because you will see them with clarity and purpose. This is the power of strategy.

Chapter IV – Strategically Adapting to Change

I commit to ADAPT to Change!

How can the M.A.I.L. principle set a new standard?

_____

_____

What is the benefit when I use the BIG Picture to lead?

_____

_____

What paradigm shifts can I make today?

_____

_____

Which of the six leadership truths apply to me?

_____

_____

Chapter IV – Strategically Adapting to Change

Chapter V – Sustainable Business Strategy

> "True change
> happens on the inside first,
> never on the outside."
>
> Mike Rodriguez

Sustainable Business Strategy

Chapter V – Sustainable Business Strategy

Resilience is such a wonderful word that is often used improperly as a platitude. It is frequently discounted or written off as a magical word for tough people; that is simply not true. Resilience comes from the Latin word 'resilire' which means to 'rebound' or 'start back.' When I think of resilience or of being resilient, I often visualize hitting a wall and falling, and thinking how it is my responsibility to connect my heart, attitude, and actions to get back up and start going again!

The truth is that we are all going to hit walls or drop in holes in life, and when we do, we will almost always fall. Walls and holes are inevitable, and falling is often the result, but to get back up and to keep going is always a choice! With holes, we can get stuck and not see the way out, but it's there if we can just rise higher to see it. We must learn that resilience is a choice!

When we choose to be resilient, we aren't focusing on the wall, the hole, or the fall. Resilient people focus on much bigger things; they focus on WHY they are doing what they are doing, and they focus on WHY they need to get back up!

The characteristics of resilient people always start with having a positive attitude, a clear purpose, shifts to focus, and ends with another action to keep going, again and again. Resilient people understand and accept that success will never come if they stop, but if they keep going, the results are potentially endless. Resilient people aren't special people, but they believe in something that is special to them. Because of that belief, they get back up to pursue it when they are knocked down. Resilience starts becoming mandatory in their lives because it becomes a part of who they are.

THE WORD 'IMPOSSIBLE'

When I was younger, I used to do things just to prove people wrong because I wanted to show them that I was capable. Now in my life, I don't seek to please people, I seek to encourage people. I challenge people to pursue what is important to them,

Chapter V – Sustainable Business Strategy

but that they might believe is impossible due to having a faulty belief system. I also challenge people to rethink the concepts of "quitting" and "failing." Quitting is a decision, usually made by people who aren't committed while failing is a result of taking an action that needs to be re-evaluated. Resilient people learn from failing, while others learn to adapt to quitting, often justifying why they quit.

When I committed to starting my speaking and training business, I was told by many people, including many well-known professional speakers and trainers, that the career was impossible to break into and that I shouldn't take the risk since I had a family. Some said I should quit, but I was determined to succeed, knowing and understanding that I would face failures. I would politely thank them and remind them that their opinion had absolutely no impact on my career outcome and that my path was unique for me. Ironically, after starting, my career actually took off within a few months. Before long I was speaking in front of crowds of hundreds and it only grew from there. Those same people are silent today.

When I went to write my first book, that same resistance showed up from a new set of people, but I stayed the course. When I faced failure and was told to give up, I got back up. Now fifteen books later and over 100,000 people trained globally, many of those same people ignore me today.

Unfortunately, success is hard for people to pursue and almost impossible for others to accept. Most people aren't against success, the truth is that most people have big dreams, but very few take action to pursue them. Whether they are afraid of failure, judgment, or they might lack confidence, or maybe even have excuses that they grew up believing, if a person has dreams that they believe are impossible, they will become impossible to them. But that isn't the biggest problem…the biggest problem can be the fallout from quitting, as those same people sometimes criticize others because they need to blame someone for their lack

Chapter V – Sustainable Business Strategy

of success. This creates a circle of negativity, anger, jealousy, and lashing out; the chronic traits of complainers. For me, my life story has been about people telling me things are impossible, that I shouldn't do certain things, or that some things just couldn't happen. I have found that when people tell you that "something is impossible," that's only what THEY believe, therefore it will be impossible for them. The better question that I ask people to evaluate is, "What do you believe?"

FIVE STEPS TO BECOME MORE RESILIENT

Everyone has access to resilience inside of them to recognize and build. Here are my five steps anyone can take to become more resilient:

1. **Recognize that you have resilience inside of you and that you can use it if you choose to.**

    Throughout my life, every time I experienced long-periods of failure, I was always not recognizing my resilience, therefore, I wasn't using it. Instead, I was focusing on failure, excuses, blame, self-pity, and other life anchors, or I was hanging around the wrong people. Lion Leaders look back on their lives and find an opportunity where they could have permanently failed, but they didn't because they kept going. They review what was going on at that time and work to apply those principles to their life today. When you can believe and accept that you do indeed have a choice about your life and business direction, you can get back up, and move to step two:

2. **Determine your BIG purpose that inspires you.**

    Purpose is the fuel that prompts you to get back up and keep going. For me, it wasn't until I figured out my true purpose that I got on track for success. I often tell people that **if you lack purpose, you will probably never get started, or if you do** get started, and your purpose isn't genuine or your own, you will probably quit when things get too tough.

Many times, I meet people who aren't succeeding because they aren't following their own dream, therefore it's not important to them. As a result, it's easier for them to give up. I was in the business world for over twenty-five years and although I never quit, I never realized my true potential. Don't get me wrong, I was very successful, but because I wasn't doing what was aligned with my heart and skillset, I wasn't using my gifts to their fullest. **When you realize what is important to you, you will remove the things that aren't important; you will accept nothing less than your purpose.**
That leads us to the next step:

3. Commit to your Big purpose.

Most people don't make commitments, simply because they don't have the right purpose or if they do commit, they won't make it public to avoid accountability in case they fail. Instead, most people use the phrase "I'll try." The truth is that you will not succeed in anything you are only 'trying to do' and you will not commit to something that isn't important to you.

When it comes to commitment, much like resilience, we must understand what the word means. My definition is that **"Commitment doesn't mean you won't fail; it means you refuse to give up. No excuses, no exit plans."** Resilience and commitment are critical components that must be present and used together by Lion Leaders.

When I started speaking, we encountered many failures as we launched, but because I was committed, we would evaluate failures and learn from them to find a new way. When you commit to something that you believe in, that's positive and good for others and this world, then you will want to keep going to create a positive impact. This type of commitment is what keeps you on track through the difficult times. **Don't try, commit, and find a way!**

4. Have faith and avoid people without it.

This is another word that is often shared as a platitude. Faith means that we are focusing on things that we do not see today, but that we know will be possible for tomorrow if we only keep going today. For me, my faith was often diluted or absent when I listened to complainers or let the negativity of others compromise my faith. Today I tell people that **others probably won't understand your dreams and goals, and that's ok, it's not for them to understand, but you better have faith if it is your dream.**

Throughout my life, I have had many distractions. Whether I was hanging out with the wrong people or group or being involved with unhealthy things, I always felt that I could do more and become more. I believe distractions are the key to failure for most leaders today. Distractions fill time, but don't help to build people up. Distractions cause most leaders to simply believe that they cannot do more or become more. It's another self-destructive lie. The people you hang out with and the things you are doing are indeed having a critical impact on your life and business. You should honestly ask yourself **"Am I growing or slowing?"** If you are slowing, then you are being distracted and you need to take action today to break free.

For every success I have had, my Christian faith has always pulled me through. Although, I have had people encouraging me, I have also had a group of people who sought to discourage me, sometimes those who were very close to me. You must have good friends, but again, look for people and mentors who will teach you, guide you, and encourage you to keep going.

5. **Don't get sidetracked; never give up.**

I made a commitment long ago that I could live with tiredness, difficulty, and hard work in order to accomplish what I have been called to do, but I also committed that I could not live with the pain of regret. I still haven't met anyone who can honestly say that they can live with regret. I came to terms with the fact that when I fell, if I didn't get back up, I could not live with the results. I could not live a life of mediocrity or failure. Therefore, I get back up. I have also committed to the fact that when you give up, not only are you choosing not to rebound, but more importantly, you are choosing not to be a better you.
The question is can you live with that decision?

FIND A WAY

One of my BIG goals is to inspire the "Find A Way!" movement for Lion Leaders to work together to eradicate negativity and complaining. I'm not saying to act like all things are wonderful all the time, but what I am saying is that all Lion Leaders should be honestly seeking to create the "find a way" mindset in their people. We should be looking for truth from our people, not complaints, they (and we) should offer solutions, not resistance, and we should stop gossiping and talking about what we don't like, but we should promote what we love and are committed to.

In today's world, too many people are focused on hate all in the name of love and they want to share that hate with everyone, all in the name of love. It's ironic and destructive chaos. Real love forgives and seeks resolution; it seeks to find a way. Whether you or someone you know is facing a difficulty or has been knocked down, and their purpose is valid and beneficial to all, as a Lion Leader, remind them that through faith and action all things are possible.

Don't complain about things or focus on what you don't like, focus on what you DO have, what you CAN do, and then

Chapter V – Sustainable Business Strategy

get it done. Negativity itself is a movement that seeks to prevent success, impede productivity, destroy faith, and create resistance. Complaining is the preferred tool of negative people to propagate anger, which holds people back and stops us from finding a way. It destroys the very idea of resilience.

We all should choose to discover our purpose, to commit to it, to create a positive impact in this world, and then to passionately pursue it while we lead and encourage others. If we want to change the world, we must first commit to changing our own lives first; we must find a way.

I CHALLENGE YOU

In a lion pride when one member decides that they want to lead, they will challenge the leader. When this happens, the challenger has reached a point in their life and in their mind that they believe they are capable, prepared, and strategically ready to lead. The only obstacle that stands in the way is their ability to defeat the existing leader. Their belief system must be validated, they will decide to pursue the coveted spot, and at some point, they will decide to utilize the power of their strategy. Today, I challenge you to replace yourself as an unbalanced leader and to choose to become a Lion Leader:

I challenge you to change your Leadership philosophy to the strategic power of the system of 3.
You have learned that any other system lacks the Power of Strategy. Lion Leaders know that they are equipped to change their perspective to move their team and their career to the next level. Lion Leaders refuse to be tactically driven. They are forward thinkers who are constantly looking to improve. They know they have greater a philosophy and a responsibility. They are not arrogant; they are humble and confident.

Chapter V – Sustainable Business Strategy

I challenge you to strategically balance your culture and performance.
Every leader is establishing these daily. Either of yours might have been holding you back, but not anymore. Commit today to seek balance. Lion Leaders take a closer look to ensure they aren't putting more time into one over the other. They recognize that just because they have been doing something for a long time that they no longer have an excuse to accept it as being 'right.' They know that just because they have been getting a good result, doesn't mean it's the best way. Lion Leaders recognize and eliminate unbalanced cultures.

I challenge you to strategically become a balanced leader.
This means that you seek to make decisions based on facts and not opinions. Lion Leaders refocus every morning and relax every night after reviewing their day. They know that if they are performing at a balanced level during challenging moments, then they don't have to worry about the opinions of everyone else. Lion Leaders don't do what is popular, they do what is right and best for the overall team. They seek to create and stay in balance.

I challenge you to tap into the strategic power of the competitor and to stay at that level.
You may be at a point in your life or career that you don't want to be. Know that you can change if you desire to. Lion Leaders have been complainers and complacent. They realized those mindsets weren't acceptable to them, so they took action to change. They like to win, and they need to win. Not for the sake of beating others, but for the sense of accomplishment and fulfillment that it brings in knowing they did their best for themselves, their family, and their team. Lion Leaders don't experience burn out, because they work, rest, and play with purpose.

Chapter V – Sustainable Business Strategy

I challenge you to claim the power of strategic thinking.
Start believing that you can become a great leader if you start doing the things required of a great leader. You may not be a strategic thinker today, but you can be if you work at it. Lion Leaders think about ways to change and improve their lives, the lives of others, and the performance of their organization. They do this by seeking facts, truth, and logic. Lion Leaders are Inside-Out Thinkers, active listeners, and effective communicators. They intentionally work on these areas.

I challenge you to no longer negotiate with mediocrity.
Lion leaders know that they set the tempo and standards for their team culture and performance. They use Q.E.S.T. to evaluate talent to bring on competitors. They train emerging leaders to become better and ensure that they have everything they need to win. Lion Leaders develop their complacent team members by helping them to realize their purpose and their potential. Lion Leaders refuse to accept excuses, blame, negativity, or mediocrity. They recognize that these are symptoms of complainers. They know that complainers create resistance, unhealthy cultures, and damage performance. Lion Leaders do not tolerate or accept anything that will compromise the success of the team member or the health of the team. Lion Leaders move people up or they move them out. They know there is no middle.

I challenge you to take action to become a resilient Lion Leader. Lion Leaders are respected, trusted, and loved by their pride; not because they are friends with everyone, but because of their positive influence. Lion Leaders help their teams to discover their courage and to shed their skins of complacency. They establish a vision and help others to realize and believe without a doubt.

Chapter V – Sustainable Business Strategy

They inspire others to pursue excellence as a team with complete and unquestioned accountability. Lion Leaders find a way when no one else can see a way. They rise after everyone else has fallen. Their power and strength are manifested in the way they carry themselves: silent and controlled power, for the betterment of the team, to pursue the vision and exceed the expectations of what they were born to do.

Never forget that leadership is a privilege and an honor that few embrace properly, but not you. Leadership requires courage and is not for the weak. Even the Bible reminds us: "To whom much is given, much will be required" (Luke 12:48). Leadership is a responsibility of authority that you have earned and that you should respect. However, it is not necessary to remind people of your authority or to reduce it in an effort to be accepted. Your leaders trust in you and placed you where they need you to be, based on your qualifications, expertise, strategic thinking, and testing.

When you apply the principles of strategy as outlined in this book, you will get resistance. Your team will struggle as they find their new vision and footing by applying new standards. After time, after challenges, and after tests of endurance by all members of the team, they will come to trust you and love you, knowing what you represent. This can only happen once your team knows that you have their best interest at heart. Don't be afraid to create disruptive change when necessary.

Some people will emotionally deflect and hide behind the false claims of their dislike for you as a leader or that your new strategic approaches are not fair. What they really dislike is the new accountability to perform and the expectations to step outside of their mediocrity. Don't give in; stretch their comfort zones. Whatever your current role is, know that you now have everything you need to start your journey towards success. You just need to recognize it and own it. As you start using the power of strategy contained in this book, you can effectively change the

Chapter V – Sustainable Business Strategy

outcome of your results, your career, the course of your life, and the lives of others.

I challenge you and ask you to embrace the power of strategy as you continue your journey to become a Lion Leader.

I have challenged you. What will you do?

ACCEPT THE CHALLENGE

I accept the challenge to become a Lion Leader:

_____
Signed

_____
Date

Chapter V – Sustainable Business Strategy

The Final Challenge

We need to continue to grow bold and fearless
Lion Leaders around the world.
We need more bold, strategic thinkers.

I challenge you to help change the course of business and the
quality of behaviors of people in the world,
one person at a time.
I am counting on you to challenge another person to become a
Lion Leader.
Let someone borrow your book or
invest in a copy for them.

I Accept This Challenge:

_____
Print YOUR Name

_____
YOUR SIGNATURE

_____
DATE

Chapter V – Sustainable Business Strategy

Chapter V – Sustainable Business Strategy

"Now, it's time for you to become a Lion Leader.

Go Forth and Make Your Life Exceptional!"
- *Mike Rodriguez*

Chapter V – Sustainable Business Strategy

Chapter V – Sustainable Business Strategy

Chapter V – Sustainable Business Strategy

Chapter VI Tips from Lion Leaders

Chapter VI   Tips from Lion Leaders

Dear Lion Leader:

As a trainer of lion leaders, I realize the importance of seeking insight from those outside of your pride, those who have navigated the terrain, made course corrections, and are pursuing success.

In this final chapter, I have asked a few that I have worked with and mentored to share their favorite leadership strategy with you. Teamwork is a foundational principle to the success of a Lion Leader.

Enjoy,

Mike

Chapter VI   Tips from Lion Leaders

"As iron sharpens iron,
so one person sharpens another."
Proverbs 27:17

VI

Tips from More Lion Leaders

Chapter VI   Tips from Lion Leaders

Narrow Your Focus
Michael Trifari – President and Chief Operating Officer, Vibe Restaurants (Little Caesars, Wingstop)

What I value the most from my career in the quick-service restaurant industry is the privilege of working alongside some of the best crews, managers, and leaders in the business. The restaurant industry, in my experience, is a great example of how people from diverse backgrounds can come together to learn from each other, work hard, celebrate success, and win as a team. I am so grateful for the feedback of everyone that took the time to share their wisdom with me as my career advanced to higher levels of accountability and influence.

Today, I strive to pay it forward and lead teams with the same passion to teach and coach for personal and professional growth that helped guide my career. One piece of advice that I believe is relevant at every level of an organization is to narrow your focus to those tasks that will deliver great results and achieve professional growth.

Most of the employees and managers that I have worked with, desire to do a good job. They care and are willing to work hard, but too often do not invest their time wisely. The restaurant business is hard work dealing with multiple priorities and distractions. I tell managers that spending a 12-hour day reacting to the symptoms of problems is exhausting work and never-ending. Narrowing your focus to work smarter is choosing to fix problems at the root cause. Taking the time to discover the root cause of a problem is to find long-term solutions that will correct a problem forever. These solutions will then become part of our systems and processes to how we execute our day-to-day standards, policies, and best practices.

As a General Manager, I spent a lot of time executing day-to-day tasks such as product prep, placing food orders, and writing crew schedules. Although having people and products to

Chapter VI   Tips from Lion Leaders

serve customers is critically important, when I still fell short of sales goals, I realized I needed to look for missed opportunities. I found that my greatest opportunities were right in front of me. The more time I spent teaching my crew and managers the day-to-day management functions and then empowered them to take the lead, the more time I eventually got back in my day.

Building a winning team ultimately allowed me the time to dig deeper into cost issues and to see my business through the customer's perception. Every minute spent narrowing my focus to improve the customer's experience by developing the capabilities of my team, in turn, became an investment in my own success as well. As a new multi-unit manager, I first attempted to lead as the general manager at all my assigned restaurants. It did not take long before I realized this approach was not working. Instead, I narrowed my focus to leveraging the strengths of each manager on my team by sharing my knowledge where I could help, while also encouraging managers to share their best practices with their peers. Creating a collaborative culture where we learn from each other helped us to exceed expectations and to win big as a team.

I focused on three main tactics to engage my managers to narrow their focus:

- Gain Commitment
- Continuous Improvement
- Celebrate Success

I found that initially, managers will do what you tell them to do for as long as you are still in the building. The key to engagement is gaining their commitment. To gain commitment, it is important to understand what existing beliefs a manager may have as a barrier to their own success. Once I understand their point of view, I can empathize and use my style of communicating which is to tell a story or verbally paint a picture. Then they see a clear path to achieving better results.

Chapter VI   Tips from Lion Leaders

Never settle for mediocrity or assume a manager is not willing to put in the effort to be the best. Leadership is inspiring continuous improvement. Keep asking the question, how can today be better than yesterday and tomorrow better than today? Celebrate the little successes to fuel enthusiasm and keep the momentum going and winning big will become contagious.

When I arrived at Vibe Restaurants in 2017, I was excited for the opportunity to make a difference as the Chief Operating Officer. I spent the first 60 days traveling to meet with directors, supervisors, and managers across eight states, observing operations, and gaining insights from frontline employees. What I discovered is that there were no clear performance expectations in terms of sales growth and individual accountability. Managers and above store leaders were in reaction mode and doing their best with limited support. Food and labor costs were a priority, but with no clear direction or support on how to manage these costs consistently and effectively.

Although there were numerous opportunities on my priority list the first step again was to narrow my focus. We created a strategic plan based on what could realistically be accomplished in year one, two, and three that would improve operations and significantly drive positive comparable sales growth, profitability, and new store development. As a result, we have added to our portfolio of restaurants 10 new locations on average each year for the past three years through new store openings and acquisitions. Having a plan for success is important but even more important is that any plan is well executed. I think some people have the perception that achieving 80% of a massive plan is a good strategy. I do not subscribe to this methodology. In my opinion, a solid plan includes realistic stretch goals that are specific and measurable and tie directly to pay, recognition, and incentive programs. Job performance is not measured by effort alone but instead, individual responsibility in executing and achieving planned objectives at the level of the organization. This level of accountability also serves to narrow the focus on how teams work together. Expectations cascade throughout the entire organization when teams collaborate to achieve common goals. We created a balanced scorecard to measure results fairly and consistently. We make the time to celebrate success through individual praise and recognition. By narrowing our focus, we are well on our way to building a culture of teamwork and servant leadership. I am so proud of all the amazing Lion Leaders I have the good fortune to learn from every day. And I look forward to the future and all the opportunities that we will achieve together.

About Michael Trifari

Michael Trifari has over 35 years of experience in the quick-service restaurant industry. He has led high performing teams in both company and franchise operations at Arby's and Burger King Corporation. As a Director of Company Operations, Michael was directly accountable for a portfolio of restaurants in North and South Carolina with annual sales exceeding $75 million in revenue. As a Director of Franchise Performance, he supported over 400 restaurants consulting with franchisees across the U.S. Michael is currently the President and Chief Operating Officer at Vibe Restaurants. Operating in 9 states, Vibe Restaurants is one of the largest franchisees of Little Caesars Pizza and a Brand Partner with Wingstop.

Chapter VI Tips from Lion Leaders

Chapter VI   Tips from Lion Leaders

Fundamental Principles are Core
Sasha Sigal – President, CTIconnect

"Keep calm and carry on," today's popular social media tagline, was actually written by the British government in preparation for World War II. How ironic is it that in 2020 we so strongly relate with this 1939 call to action, when strategic leaders were planning a mental mindset before going into one of the most impactful battles of world history? The message and its intent are timeless, surviving multi-generational societal change as a modern beacon of social media propaganda. Planning for a goal is imperative because the truth is, nothing worthwhile happens by accident.

As an active believer of the power in the peace of mind, I revert to a daily practice of intention setting as a necessity, not an option. A mentor once told me, however, that unintended consequences are inevitable when the intention is not met with strategy. In other words, short cuts rarely form long term solutions as even the smallest of goals need proper planning for successful execution. If you are an impatient leader, the perceived "rub" is defining time as a wasted financial asset, especially when the goal is seemingly attainable without spending time planning it. A simple change in perception by acknowledging that time is now invested for the greater good rather than wasted, will only accelerate momentum during the implementation phase.

As someone who is inherently impulsive, the importance of stopping time to not only set a goal, but identify pain points in advance of goal implementation, allows for a strong mindset even when navigating through the pain. While the metric of time is specific to the goal, efficient execution is probable when a leader optimizes the strengths of the team and makes confident decisions for resolution. However, there is a fine line between confidence and impulsion. Confident decisions are a result of

Chapter VI Tips from Lion Leaders

preparation coupled with understanding a detailed scope of work, while impulsion is a desire for instant gratification ultimately driven by impatience. Therefore, I make every intention with a positive mindset. I practice a fundamental process which produces additional confidence that every challenge has a resolution. Knowing that any challenge has absolute resolve allows for a subconscious composure when faced with adversity. In my case, consistency in mindful positive intention coupled with a focus on a stable foundation opened doors in my career much sooner than initially expected. That is the beauty of strategy, the result of execution may exceed your expectation, but the art of navigating momentum is a process made possible with a strong fundamental foundation.

When I think about the path of my career, I recognize that every goal I set, irrespective of size, was followed by a recipe of evolving fundamental principles. The most recent example of strategic implementation was in December of 2019 when I accepted the role as the President of a Florida based wireless hardware distributor, CTIconnect. The first step was once again to set a positive intention for our future (the big picture): to acquire exponential revenue growth while enhancing the customer experience, simultaneously transforming the culture by instilling trust and confidence in my team with clear goals, strategic planning, and systematic change they can feel.

The employee experience is as important to me as the customer experience, so I wanted to ensure my entire team was involved in every part of our evolution from the very beginning to enhance a vested interest in growing together. I had to understand the culture before assuming I needed to change it, so my first sub intention was set and I hit the ground running by pressing on the obvious pain: revenue target attainment in an effort to test their aptitude for pressure knowing that this would soon be their new normal. After all, it was the last few weeks of the year, so I set a revenue target never before achieved by this

Chapter VI   Tips from Lion Leaders

team. I laid out a script of tactical behaviors for the team to follow through year-end to optimize their capabilities coupled with motivational and transparent "can-do" communication. I held them accountable for every directive as we neared the edge of 2020. I knew that telling them to do it was only something they were accustomed to, so I shared insight on the "how," the strategy. The smaller goal was to show they were capable and with behavioral tweaks and trust in the process, an unattainable goal was possible...even in two short weeks. It was an aggressive approach, but I knew they could do it and now I convinced them they could too as we cheered in awe of their accomplished target. The energy was electric as the clock struck midnight to a new year and they passed the test as a powerful team. It was now time to include them in the next sub intention for finding the root cause of internal issues. We needed to secure a foundation strong enough to uphold the desired exponential growth.

The company already had the proper basic tools within, but they were underutilized. They were wrapped in years of learned complacent behaviors and self-reliance caused by distrust from a high leadership turn rate. My prediction was that a pattern would identify itself to me as they submitted complaints from every division in the company. My path was now well-identified and imbedded with pain as I gathered the team for our first Townhall Meeting. This was only a short three weeks after their end of year win. The purpose was to share the analysis of a proposed strategy built in a 30, 60, 90-day segment highlighting resolve for their communicated pain. Once again, communicating short term goals for a long-term intention.

In addition, the 3-day session was inclusive of training highlighted around the pattern I found in their submitted communications. This was followed by a series of 1x1 meetings to uncover any obstacles not yet identified and a plan to expose the strength of each individual in the company. While the initial meeting set the tone for 2020, I also knew that consistency was

Chapter VI   Tips from Lion Leaders

going to be key for this group as their history was riddled with an ever-present change. As the year progressed, difficult decisions were inescapable as some didn't make it through the transition but staying on course was imperative. New hires were placed strategically in positions of their strengths and in alignment with company needs. Teamwork and delegation are absolute mandates in my fundamental process. Identifying the strength of my team exposed an opportunity to unify our company. We did this by optimizing the work they loved while implementing change openly in organizational structure without hesitation. The exercise of strength optimization is a continuous effort as is the practice of setting sub intentions. The exercise also exposed unexpected leadership opportunities for my team. Its also exposed and a new path for evolving desired career goals allowing for a new wave of positive energy.

Today our team is thriving in unity with high morale and a trajectory for 40% YoY growth, surpassing targets previously deemed impossible. We are rebuilding everything from process to our mission statement as one. The long-term goal remains the same, but the sub intentions are molded as we progress into a new era together. In reality, the change in their perception of what is possible was created with an initial and repetitive communication of a long-term goal. It was broken down into smaller feasible intentions that continue to prove the impact of a fundamental system of processes. This includes patience, transparency, optimization of a team, and an ever-present positive mindset.

Mike Rodriguez once told me "It is not about what happened, it's your response that matters." I carry these words with me as I maintain unequivocally positive in my intention to build something spectacular our entire company can be proud to say is accomplished in teamwork and dedication to our mission.

Chapter VI   Tips from Lion Leaders

About Sasha Sigel

Sasha Sigal is the President of CTIconnect, a leading distributor of fixed wireless and telecommunications infrastructure. Since joining the company in December of 2019, Sigal generated over 30% revenue growth and redesigned company vision using 15 years of experience in Sales and Operations to drive focus in the top and bottom line optimization through strategic process implementation, corporate morale initiatives, and transparent communication. Her drive for efficiency and optimizing the strength of her team corresponds with a relentless desire to simultaneously enhance the experience of both customers and employees.

Chapter VI   Tips from Lion Leaders

Chapter VI   Tips from Lion Leaders

Leadership Love
David Rodriguez -Owner / Operator, Chick-Fil-A

Our purpose is to "Love people and have fun while serving them excellence!" We intentionally set our company purpose to be direct and short. It best serves our team and adds value, encompassing so much in a short statement. Love is a universally accepted value, but love can be an incredibly awkward word. It has the potential to be received in a clunky, uncomfortable manner. However, as lion leaders, if we speak to love immediately and confidently, it sets the tone for the organization. It is a risk to a leader. My experience is that the benefits far outweigh the risk. Not one person on our team nor one of our guests or vendors has ever declined to receive love. To show understanding, kindness, goodness, and a desire to get to know another team member is really simple and rewarding. Being that simple and focused makes life better.

It is quite possible that you may know a person who has never been loved well. Not everyone has acted in a manner of love. Not everyone knows how to love another human being on Planet Earth. That, however, is where we have an incredible opportunity. It is possible that they may want to receive that manner of treatment and feel accepted. Not knowing how to love or not knowing how to receive love is completely acceptable on our team. It is never forced.

One of the many things I learned from Mike Rodriguez, was to clearly set expectations. We describe expectations while onboarding our team on how to treat fellow team members and how to treat our guests. This requires an investment of time, one that always feels expensive and time-consuming. However, perceptions of the benefits of an intangible concept such as love, especially inside a for-profit business, may be deceiving. From my personal experience, it has required us to operate out of our comfort zone and required conversations that take time. There

Chapter VI   Tips from Lion Leaders

are several instances where an employee has quit and pursued another job. It does not always work. It is not always respected. It is always remembered.

Building an organization with the practical approach of love has completely been a game-changer for us. Our ability to speak in love and speak to a person's worth directly, regardless of performance, has been liberating. Our team's security is strong. Their acceptance of one another is high. The team's willingness to grow is amazing. Our ability to ask for and receive performance improvement has been incredibly encouraging. There is a trust that is both spoken to and understood. Our ability to hold our team accountable, improve performance results, and create a sustainable culture has been rewarding. Once the intent of love inside a business organization is understood, we then speak to Truth, Trust, and Relationship.

Truth. We ask that we only speak the truth to each other, especially in the little events. If we can build trust and accountability, even in the small things, then we earn the possibility of building trust in the large, eye-catching events. The fear that many new members and leaders have is that if they speak the truth then they will push people away or risk losing their job. Imagine that for a minute. There is a fear that if they are truthful; it is a risk to them. If done rudely or offensively, yes, this can be true. It would be a risk to speak truth if the leader is not responsible with the truth. Can we as leaders allow and even afford for fear like that to be greater than a sense of security or trust?

As a leader, if you flinch, move off-center, or overreact, your moment of truth is lost with that person and your ability to earn trust is lost. Yes, just in one moment. Yet, when the truth is spoken out of love and done so relative to our common expectations, we actually raise awareness as a team. Not just for those in the conversation, but the rest of the team observes positive changes, and our overall performance increases. Our

Chapter VI   Tips from Lion Leaders

biggest failures and our biggest wins have not just been with the team members, but with the stadium full of observers that want to know how the leader will handle "this one."

When we can be consistent in speaking truth to each other, our trust in each other increases, not decreases. We are encouraging faith and love in each other, not fear of each other. As our truth with each other and our trust in each other increases, we naturally experience an increase in our relationships as well. In these relationships, we tend to have more fun, be more creative, help each other, look out for each other, and serve each other better. As these relationships strengthen, our willingness to go the second mile together becomes more enjoyable. The long, hard days that do come are made better, not worse, with relationships built on truth and trust.

This is not easy. It is simple! Getting to the truth together and operating in love takes consistent work. The work is not hard, just uncomfortable. It requires changing habits, time, and intentionality. It requires a focus that is not self-centered, but others-centered. The benefits are amazing - lives well lived with others. Would you choose love if you knew you couldn't fail?

About David Rodriguez

David is the Owner/Operator of Chick-fil-A Hwy 210 & Ayala, located in Rialto, California. Born in Richardson, Texas, Dave earned the Eagle Scout Award at 16 years of age. He received the Presidential Scholarship Award from Texas A&M University in College Station, Texas. He earned the position of Company Commander of his Navy/Marine

Chapter VI   Tips from Lion Leaders

Corps of Cadet Unit and served a unit of 60 men while earning a Bachelor of Arts in Business Administration. He later earned an MBA from the University of Dallas. Dave was blessed with the opportunity to serve some amazing domestic and international corporations in several industries such as natural gas, electricity, telecommunications, and lean manufacturing. Today, Dave leads a growing team of approximately 120 employees who love and serve the Rialto Communities. His purpose is to raise leaders of character for the city, state, and nation. Dave and his wife Lisa, have two daughters and live in their country home in Southern California.

Chapter VI   Tips from Lion Leaders

In Support of Lion Leadership
Kelly Stephens – Vice President
Engel & Volkers

What does being a Lion Leader mean to me? Let's first talk about "Leader." I have found the word Leader to take on a broader meaning. Leading is all about finding people who want to follow you. Not that you drag them along. So how have I found it helpful to "get" people to follow me? There are a few key components for sure! Trust, respect, honor, and courage are four points that I want to share with you. What do those mean when you are a leader and how do each of those become "Lion" Leader traits?

First, there is trust – your team or pack needs to know where you are coming from, your experience, your background, your "heart." How does a lion earn its position in their pack? Do they show they are fearless and skilled? Of course they do. So, your team might be thinking, "Who are you?" or "Why should I listen to you much less let you lead me?" You also have to consider that, as a businessperson, all of your business is online! The people that are about to work for you will hear your name and immediately Google you. Have you googled yourself? That exercise can be quite eye-opening but one step that you don't want to miss. Make sure you know what they are going to find and that you will be seen online as a leader that they now look forward to meeting in person. What do your reviews say about you? Have you solicited LinkedIn or other testimonials in the past? What will they find out about you that shares with them what others say about the experience of working with you? It's easy to teach yourself, but what matters, even more, is what others have to say, right?

As for Trust, we know that is earned or expanded over time too. But what can you do upfront to earn some immediate trust? Do what you say you are going to do is a good way to start.

Chapter VI Tips from Lion Leaders

Also, understanding that people are usually resistant to change, so maybe being an observer at first and really understanding the dynamics of the team would lead them to understand that you do care and are there for them. Not just to come in and make changes to "stroke an ego."

I have found the best transitions to be, when I made time to really get to know everyone personally. When I made individual appointments, even if just for 10 minutes, to find out about that employee. Who is their family, who is important to them, why do they work there, what is their "Why," what is their biggest hurdle at work? And what is their greatest reward? Kind of like a Lion waking to the jungle in the morning. He first stands tall, and then looks around. What is different in the landscape? Is that difference, friend, foe, or food? Great questions for the Lion to access how the morning is going to start. All great questions as a leader so that you can get to know the team and what is important to them as a person.

Understanding why your team is there and doing what they are currently doing is important in showing that you care and that you are also a team player, not just the leader. This will earn you trust and help move toward the Respect quotient.

Respect is next. Respect is why people CONTINUE to follow you. If you lose respect, you probably have a disgruntled employee that is just waiting for that next opportunity to come along, so they can leave. Are they looking for another Lion that is stronger or more skilled to get behind? Respect is best shown in communication, communication verbally, body language, online, and in any written communications. Communicating the rules, the expectations, the goals, the rewards, and the levels of achievement met with certain goals. And of course, making sure those are fair to all involved and that favoritism is never happening. Impartial and Fair...Impartial and Fair....as a leader you have to make hard decisions even when it comes to the people that, personally, you might connect better with or favor

Chapter VI Tips from Lion Leaders

(if favoritism were allowed). In the jungle, it really is life or death. In business, it is success or failure. When people feel like they understand what is expected and that everyone is treated equally, they work harder and better. There is purpose and passion behind what they are doing. And if you found out in the first meeting what is important to THEM, then you can tie those together for that employee. Tie what you want to achieve with what that employee needs to get out of it. It's a Win-Win. Mission accomplished, right?!

When you can make your goals and your employee's goals line up, you will find Honor in being their leader. They will want to work for you and help you accomplish your goals. The greatest leaders of our Nation had Honor behind them. Honor is defined as, respect with the highest regard. If you think of someone you honor, there is a sense of pride that swells up inside you. We see Lions as proud and regal, so that is why we call them a pride. You want that sense of belonging for your team and what you want them to go home at night with is that feeling about you. That feeling that they are working hard for a greater good and purpose.

The fourth one is probably the hardest. Courage – the King of the Jungle! The cowardly lion is only true in the Wizard of Oz! It takes courage to lead people because the buck stops with you. You are making decisions that impact many. You are answering the tough questions, phone calls, complaints, etc. You have to stay courageous and strong during those interactions. Think of how the Lion became known as the King of the Jungle. Noticeably, the Lion has a strong respect for an elephant. But they know their respective power. You will be called for courage when a new tactic is employed that hasn't been tried before. You might have to "get out of the box". Your front line and hierarchy of leadership is your strength. Have the courage to empower those on your team. The positions within your group will be your defensive and offensive strategy as you go about your day in the

Chapter VI   Tips from Lion Leaders

jungle that you call work/life. Understanding and harnessing the power of those on your team helps to give strength to the whole group. This strength and understanding help the entire organization grow and feel powerful!

Trust the team to get you to where you want the company to go! Show them that they can trust you to help guide them there. Show them respect. They will respect you. Honor your promises and company standards. Have the courage to be their Lion Leader. Think of the true leaders of your past. Think of what made them great leaders. Take that same courage to lead your team with trust, respect, and honor as you have appreciated in your career. People make the difference. People want those 3 things in every facet of their lives. Work is no different than a relationship. You have a relationship with those under you to lead them. Is your jungle terrifying or are you the King of your Jungle?

About Kelly Stephens

I have had my Real Estate License since 1994. I am a native Georgian and a 1993 graduate of The University of Georgia. I earned my Real Estate License soon after graduation. Since 1998, I have concentrated my career in Metro Atlanta. In the Fall of 2016, I joined Engel & Volkers and License Partner Shirley Gary. I presently serve as the Vice President and Managing Broker for the Buckhead Atlanta and Atlanta North Fulton offices. We have over 100 agents on our roster and represent over $300 million in annual sales volume. I joined Coldwell Banker in January 2003 and quickly rose to the level of Sales

Chapter VI   Tips from Lion Leaders

Manager. I was named the #1 New Homes Sales Agent for the Atlanta Board of Realtors in 2010 and was the #1 Sales Agent (GCI), in 2010, for Coldwell Banker NRT On-Site Agents and in the Top 1% of CB Agents Nationwide. I am a lifetime member of the Atlanta Board of Realtors Multi-Million Dollar Sales Club and a Phoenix Recipient. Throughout the years, I have served on many committees.

    I got my Brokers license and was Branch Manager and then Managing Broker for Coldwell Banker Residential Brokerage Atlanta (NRT owned) from 2012-2014; I have also served as Qualifying Broker/Sales and Marketing Manager for a mid-sized builder; overseeing all Sales and Marketing efforts for their approximate 150 New Builds annually.

Chapter VI Tips from Lion Leaders

Chapter VI   Tips from Lion Leaders

Final Words from Mike

Throughout my life and career in business, I have always enjoyed being a leader, but I was not always in pursuit of becoming a Lion Leader; mostly because I was my biggest obstacle. I was often distracted by doing things my way or by people and things that kept me from stepping into my full potential. I knew there was a "bigger picture," I just wasn't focused enough to see it. I was an authoritative leader early in my career. I led with a heavy hand and managed irresponsibly. As a result, I dealt with the repercussions of sporadic performance, lack of engagement, and high turnover. I decided to take action and improve when I chose to be aware of my ineffective skills and to seek out guidance from mentors. I came to understand the purpose of being an effective leader, and I became stronger than ever. Not in a controlling way, but in a humbled position of silent, disciplined strength.

I have learned, through failure and success, that I must be healthy in three categories: spiritually, mentally, and physically. These core life components will always be works in progress for me. However, I am committed, as I know that is how I can help and influence others. With regards to success, I have always felt that my purpose was to help others through the gift of words and speech.

I have always dreamed of becoming a professional speaker and trainer, but for the largest part of my life, I only considered this a dream. Who was I to accomplish this? This was a negative thought that I burdened myself with. So, who am I? I am a son of our King. I know Him, and He knows me. Today, all because of Him, and through my obedience, I am living my life's dream, my life's goal, and most importantly, my life's purpose. Discover God, believe in and receive Jesus and accept Him and His plan for your life. Have faith and take action. You too can become a Lion Leader.

Chapter VI Tips from Lion Leaders

Lion Leadership: The POWER of Strategy

Lion Leadership: The POWER of Strategy

About the Author

"Don't put limits on the big plans God has for your life."

MIKE RODRIGUEZ is a professional speaker, a leadership expert, and a life and business strategist. He is the founder and CEO of Mike Rodriguez International, LLC a global speaking and training firm. Mike is also a multi-Best-Selling author, with many of his books featured at Barnes & Noble book events. He is a highly sought-after advisor and trainer working with many organizations globally. Mike has co-hosted training alongside the legendary Tom Hopkins, and he is a former showcase speaker with the world-famous Zig Ziglar Corporation. In fact, he was selected as the featured speaker and sales expert for the 2015 Ziglar U.S. Tour.

Mike has been featured on CBS, U.S. News & World Report, Fast Company, Success Magazine, Authority Magazine, and many more. He has lectured at many universities including Baylor University, UNT, Louisiana Tech, UGA, K-State Research, and others. His clients include names like Bank of America, Hilton, McDonald's Corporation, Reuters News, the Federal Reserve Bank, the U.S. Army, and many others in technology and software around the world. As a master trainer, Mike has worked with and trained over a hundred thousand people around the world in a variety of countries.

Mike is a high-energy leader who worked in corporate America for close to three decades training, building, mentoring, and developing top-performing people and teams. Mike started as a struggling sales representative, with no experience or formal training. He worked his way up to become a top-performer and an award-winning sales leader. He credits his faith, having a strategic plan, taking action, and never giving up to be able to prevail over many failures and adversities in his own life. Most importantly, he has always believed in his God-given potential.

Throughout his career, Mike has built productivity-driven training programs and managed multi-million-dollar quotas. He has experience delivering powerful messages and creating personal development strategies for new and tenured companies and teams across many industries. Mike believes if you have the right attitude, you can have the right kind of success, regardless of the type of industry that you are in. He has been happily married since 1991 to the love of his life, and together they have five beautiful daughters. As of 2021, Mike and his wife will become grandparents.

Mike believes in personal development and continued education without limitations. One of his many principles is "You don't find time, you create time." He has created time to study in the higher education programs listed below, while being married, leading his family, managing two businesses, and writing books.

- Christian Leadership (MACL studies) at DTS
- Harvard University School of Business online
- Baylor Truett Seminary (Cert. of Studies)
- Study Abroad in Oxford University (Philosophy)
- Master's Degree (MDiv) at SWBTS, and
- He will finalize his Doctorate in 2023

If Mike can create time, then you can too.

Lion Leadership: The POWER of Strategy

As a top-ranked speaker, advisor,
business and life strategist,
and a leadership expert,
Mike has experience working with people
from all backgrounds and countries, personally and
professionally, all around the world.

You can schedule Mike Rodriguez
to speak or train at your next event.
Go to:
www.MikeRodriguezInternational.com

Some other books available by Mike Rodriguez:

Lion Leadership: Teamwork, Strategy, Vision
Finding Your WHY
8 Keys to Exceptional Selling
Break Your Routines to Fix Your Life
NOW Is the Best Time
Think BIG Motivational Quotes
Walking with Faith
A Bigger Purpose
Pursuing Success
Trusting in Him

Audio Courses (MP3/CD) Available from:
Nightingale Conant and Audible:

What's Holding Me Back
Finding Your WHY

Lion Leadership: The POWER of Strategy

Lion Leadership: The POWER of Strategy

Lion Leadership: The POWER of Strategy

Lion Leadership: The POWER of Strategy

Lion Leadership: The POWER of Strategy

Disclaimer & Copyright Information

The information contained in this book should not be considered legal advice. Please consult your corporate counsel or legal advisor for any matter(s) that you have questions about.

Some of the events, locales, and conversations have been recreated from memories. In order to maintain their anonymity, in some instances, the names of individuals and places have been changed. As such, some identifying characteristics and details may have changed.

Although the authors and publishers have made every effort to ensure that the information in this book was correct at press time, the authors and publishers do not assume and hereby disclaim any liability to any party for any loss, damage, or disruption caused by errors or omissions, whether such errors or omissions result from negligence, accident, or any other cause.

All quotes, unless otherwise noted,
are attributed to Mike Rodriguez or the contributing authors

Cover illustration, book design, and production
Copyright © 2021 by Tribute Publishing LLC
www.TributePublishing.com

"Go Forth and Make Your Life Exceptional" ™
and "Go Forth and Sell Something!" ™
are copyrighted trademarks of the Author, Mike Rodriguez.

Lion Leadership: The POWER of Strategy

Lion Leadership: The POWER of Strategy

I can do ALL THINGS through Christ
who strengthens me.
Philippians 4:13

Lion Leadership: The POWER of Strategy

………..now go forth and become a Lion Leader.

Lion Leadership: The POWER of Strategy

NOTES

NOTES

NOTES

www.ingramcontent.com/pod-product-compliance
Lightning Source LLC
Chambersburg PA
CBHW021105080526
44587CB00010B/397